Ms Kilpatrick
I pray this blesses your
life. Thank you for all
you do for LMPS students
and especially for my dear
children ♡

Waiting – I Hate It!

Lessons Learned Waiting on God

Kaitrin E. Valencia, Esq.

Kaitrin E Valencia

♡ Psalm 46:10 ♡

Waiting – I Hate It! Lessons Learned While Waiting on God

KDP Publishing, Independent Publishing Platform, Printed in the United States of America

1. Skyway Railroad, *Voices Outside the Stadium,* Chapter 5: Hotel and Brothel Outreach, pages 28-30, On-Demand Publishing, LLC, 2018.
2. Brown, Les. *Live Your Dreams,* Chapter 3: The Power To Change, page 75, William Morrow and Company, New York, 1992.
3. Smith, Michael W. *Surrounded (Fight My Battles).* Surrounded. Rocketown Records. February 23, 2018. MP3
4. Camp, Jeremy. *Same Power.* I Will Follow. Capital Christian Music Group. February 3, 2015. MP3
5.TobyMac. *Speak Life.* Eye On It. Forefront Records. August 28, 2012. MP3.
6. Chapman, Gary D. *The 5 Love Languages.* Chicago: Northfield Pub., 2015.
7. "Stewardship." *Merriam-Webster.com, 2019.* Web 14 January, 2019.
8. "Lamenting." *Merriam-Webster.com, 2019.* Web 14 January, 2019.

Cover Design by Imelda Valencia Cuevas

ISBN 978-1-733-5528-0-6

DEDICATION

I dedicate this book to my family and church: my husband, my children, my parents, my sister Jennifer, and First Assembly of Memphis.

I'm grateful for all the wisdom instilled from my parents that made a lot of the lessons learned in this book possible.

I am especially grateful for my husband (Emilio) and children (Noah, Kailah, and David) for all the sacrifices made during the extended time I worked on this labor of love. My husband worked multiple jobs to support our family, while I was off work writing and was often awakened at all hours of the night with me getting out of bed with sudden flashes of inspiration. Thank you for being patient and always believing in me, even when I didn't.

I am blessed with an amazing support team at our church – from all the women in my Tuesday prayer group, to my senior Pastor, Dr. Tom Lindberg – all of whom nursed me back to strength during a difficult time in my life. I am eternally grateful for your prayers, encouragement and empowerment to walk in all of God's promises.

Lastly, I can't forget my Chicago church family at New Life Covenant Church, where we served for decades. Pastor Choco, Elizabeth, and Efrain your leadership in our lives instilled a unique DNA that carries your fingerprints wherever we serve. Te amo mucho.

TABLE OF CONTENTS

Dedication

Foreward

Introduction   **1**

Part One	**The Two Great Encounters**	**8**
Chapter 1	The First Great Encounter: Cutting out Sin	9
Chapter 2	The First Great Encounter: Learning from Snags	15
Chapter 3	The Second Great Encounter: Vision	22
Chapter 4	The Second Great Encounter: Purposeful Design	30
Part Two	**Waiting and Preparing**	**39**
Chapter 5	Defining the War	39
Chapter 6	Battle Perspective	48
Chapter 7	Childlike Faith	55
Chapter 8	Weapons of Mass Destruction	62
Chapter 9	Warring to Maturity	70
Chapter 10	Avoiding Pit Stops	75
Chapter 11	Walking Confidently and Humbly	81
Chapter 12	Warring through Loneliness	88
Chapter 13	Breaking through Offenses	92
Chapter 14	Bouncing Back	99
Chapter 15	The Art of Ignoring	106
Chapter 16	Who I Really Am	111

Chapter 17	Hold on to the Promises	115
Chapter 18	Character Counts	120
Chapter 19	Personal Stewardship and Stewarding Others	136
Chapter 20	Working through the Wait	143
Chapter 21	Having the Right Posture to Hear from God	149
Chapter 22	Discerning God's Voice	155
Chapter 23	Silent Years	160
Chapter 24	Dreams, Visions, and Audible Voice	166
Part Three	**The Art of Rest**	**174**
Chapter 25	The Art of Rest	174
Part Four	**Knowing your Exit**	**183**
Chapter 26	Knowing your Exit: Uncomfortable Nest	183
Chapter 27	Knowing your Exit: God's Perfect Timing	190
	Appendix	**198**
	About the Author	**199**

FOREWORD

It is with great delight that I write the forward to this much-needed book. Kaitrin Valencia is one of my church members and I know her well. She is a mover and a shaker with a very large heart for God. Here, with clear and compelling words, she presents profound truth drawn from Scripture and off the anvil of her own experiences.

Waiting —I Hate It! comes from the soul of a woman on a mission. This book is not a lullaby to put you to sleep; it's a trumpet blast from the Holy Spirit to wake you up.

Kaitrin Valencia focuses on four seasons of life every eager Christian goes through when they desire God to use them and to develop their character. Those four seasons are...

- Two Great Encounters
  - Waiting and Preparing
    - The Art of Resting (and it is an art)
      - Knowing When To Exit (when to get up and go)

She addresses each of those four issues in a biblical and practical manner. This book is memorable, usable, and doable.

Every reader will benefit greatly from her chapter on "The Art Of Ignoring." Too many people listen way too much to the words from others. Her section on "Waiting and Preparing" is worth the price of the book. When you read and reflect on that section, you'll think, "I wish I would have had this information ten years ago."

There's no doubt every reader of this fine volume will be both motivated and inspired. This book burns with Bible fire that leaps from its page right into the reader's heart. My prayer is for God to use this book widely and start a fire of revival. This is the kind of book one will want to pass on to a friend after having read it. I commend it to you with my whole heart.

Dr. Tom Lindberg, D. Min.
Lead Pastor
First Assembly of God
Memphis, Tennessee
Adjunct Professor
Global University

INTRODUCTION
Setting the Stage

If you love waiting, raise your hand. I doubt many books dropped in affirmation. If you're anything like me, you've been on the same emotional roller coaster, too: holding pattern, being still, feeling stuck, wanting to take a shortcut, silence, stagnancy, frustration, feeling lazy and unproductive, ambiguity and not knowing or understanding the full picture, overstepping God, impatience, fear. Then, like a bolt it comes – radical faith, illogical and not making sense! Yet the peace descends upon you like feathers.

I've experienced all of these often during the waiting periods of life. Waiting for a degree, waiting to buy a house, waiting for a spouse and then waiting for children, above all, waiting for that dream to unfold for what I've been called to do.

Sometimes I've waited well and other times I've failed miserably. Yet, there's hope. I've gotten better at waiting the more I practice. How ironic that time made me better at waiting!

Time also gave me a greater appreciation for the things I was waiting for. We've all met people who get everything handed to them...those who don't know the art of waiting, working, or persevering for something. Quite frankly, some of them can be obnoxious to be around. Compared with that, there's something so endearing about being in the company of someone who knows how to wait well. They are peaceful. They are restful. They aren't anxious, uptight, constantly complaining, or throwing a tantrum when they don't get their way.

While I hate waiting, I now understand the value of waiting for something in my future. Imagine not having anything to wait for! While waiting can be agonizing, it also carries the hope of greater things to come. When I received the things I was promised (that degree, house, spouse, children, dream job), God didn't stop there. With each experience He revealed new heights for the next waiting period. Waiting has taught me to always be in a place of expectation.

Life is full of waiting and entering, waiting and entering, so we need to learn the art of mastering it. Unfortunately, the more we kick and scream during the wait, the longer we'll probably have to wait. My prayer is through our journey together we will learn ways to not circumvent the process and avoid the pitfalls of impatience, compromise, and settling for less. I am proof it is possible for a person with impatient DNA tendencies to wait well.

And there's great news! God has a lot to say about waiting. In fact, the word wait (in all its forms) is found 161 times in the Bible.

Grandfather Crank
I've always loved clocks, yet despised waiting. Oh, the irony

given clocks represent time!

My adoration for clocks stems from all the nostalgic memories of winding our grandfather clock with my father. Our weekend winding routine passed down to his grandchildren. All eleven grandchildren have pictures with their Opa, my father, proudly holding them while their little hands wound the clock key, enabling another week to be measured on the clock dial.

Clocks represent the continuum of time. Tick, tock, tick, tock. They create methodical and evenly-spaced sounds. Our family's grandfather clock has always been prominently placed in the living room, making a nap difficult due to its loud ticking and donging every quarter hour and hour. However, with time, the melodious noises became second nature to our home. I can hear the chimes of that old clock right now.

Grandfather clocks require action to stay in synchrony with our continuum of time. The crank key must be turned every week to ensure it continues functioning. While different people throughout the years have turned our family's crank key, every turn represented a continued passing of time we experienced together.

With each turn of our crank, there were celebrations: graduations, weddings, births of children. With each turn, there were hardships: death, divorces, miscarriages. Each completed rotation of the crank was accompanied by waiting for the next week's re-wind. And between each crank twist, I learned wisdom only time can produce.

As an avid genealogist, my father's desire is to pass down our family's grandfather clock and the crank from generation to generation. In the same way, my prayer is this book will pass down some wisdom I gleaned through the expanse of waiting for God's purpose and destiny to unfold.

The birth pains to document these lessons were a labor of love and at times intimidating. Ultimately, I pray the insights will help keep you focused and holding on to all God has for you during lonely, confusing, and strenuous waiting periods. You've been saturated with prayer, and I'm excited to take this journey with you.

Whatever we do, let's not put the crank down and let the clock stop ticking. We've all wanted to quit. Let's get our crank winders out, spin the clock together, and live every minute God has ordained with intentionality to its fullest capacity. Let's go!

Listening Ear and Radical Faith

> "I've given you this position of authority; what
> are you doing with it?"
> Signed, God

Chicago. May 2012. I was sitting in a management meeting in the United State's first and largest juvenile court. The city I love and call home was quickly deteriorating to drugs, gangs, and gun violence. A travesty we are becoming notorious for in the eyes of the world, as we watch a generation of our youth being senselessly killed.

The frigid Chicago winter weather began to subside and warmer air was settling in. Yet, warm air meant one thing in Chicago's juvenile justice world: more people congregating outside, equating to more violence. At the time of this management meeting, I was the youngest and least tenured person to hold a top administrative position and was a right-hand person to the director.

On this particular day at the office, a community organization was sharing the summer programs they would facilitate in efforts to keep our delinquent kids safe. As they discussed the usual summer basketball camps, inside, I tried not to feel cynical. Not because I didn't believe in sports giving young people a way out. But because for years I had watched millions of dollars being thrown at problems in a political environment.

I was tired of putting band-aids on gaping wounds knowing that, without Christ, a long-term change wasn't sustainable. For 17 years I had the cure for an epidemic terminal disease and wasn't able to share it with anyone, all the while watching people die.

And that's when it happened! I heard an internal voice ask: "I've given you this position of authority; what are you doing with it?" I didn't know how to respond to this challenge: but one thing was for sure, I didn't want to ignore it.

As I prayed for clarity, I knew God wanted to boldly empower His church to be part of the solution to our city's pervasive violence. In the coming months, I started to develop relationships with churches in our most vulnerable communities and implemented our system's first faith-based initiatives. As a result of listening to that voice challenging me to use my influence to advance the Kingdom of God, we were experiencing testimonies with our most at-risk and violent youth.

Shortly after these major milestones, I got a life-altering call from my pastor that changed the trajectory for our family. In the pinnacle of my juvenile court career, my church asked me to become the executive director of our nonprofits – something I had waited ten years to hear.

Rewind. Ten years earlier, when I got God's assignment, I was a juvenile probation officer in law school. Leaving then would've seemed easy. I didn't have much to sacrifice. But

God, in His infinite wisdom, knew I didn't possess all the skills or have the required character needed for the full-time ministry assignment. When my pastor called ten years later, I was making six figures and being groomed to become our department's next director. There were huge sacrifices in making the switch.

I'll share more details later but, for purposes of setting the stage, the overarching lessons are: (1) waiting takes sacrifice and (2) when we finally arrive at our long-awaited destination, it will inevitably require great sacrifice to step into the fullness of what we were ultimately waiting.

It was a life-changing decision when I got that call to let go of my title and financial security. I'd worked hard and surrendered much. Yet, filled with a God-sized vision, our family gave two weeks' notice and – BAM – just like that we were transitioned into full-time ministry. A pin drop could be heard in the room the day I made the announcement at juvenile court. I sensed the utter shock and disbelief.

Are you struggling with not knowing God's plan for your life? Or maybe you know His plan, but for years felt stuck in a holding pattern? Are you readily able to hear and discern the voice of God or do you question what His perfect will is with life choices? Are other's oppression, maltreatment, and slander discouraging you and interfering with your vision of God's will? Does living a God-sized dream trigger insecurity and fear?

If any of these challenges have quickened your Spirit, welcome to a self-reflective process of pushing through and experiencing the life you were born to live. No matter what our stage, the wisdom gleaned throughout this book will keep us moving toward all of God's promises and dreams while remaining in readiness. When the day comes where the waiting is over, we'll need to be ready and equipped.

Waiting isn't always easy. There are many temptations to settle or give up. God will grace us for each crucial season that I've organized into four parts of this book:

1. **The Two Great Encounters**: The personal encounter with a Savior who forgives our iniquities and receiving the revelation of God's specific purpose for our lives.

2. **Waiting and Preparing:** The arduous and sometimes lengthy process of waiting for God's call on our lives to manifest.

3. **The Art of Rest:** Being intentional about rest while in the midst of transitions.

4. **Knowing Your Exit:** The transition from the waiting period to living our destiny.

Because this is a book about waiting, we'll spend the longest time in Part Two.

The final part of the journey, not contemplated in this book, is after we exit the waiting season and begin living in God's assignment. Here we experience the fullness of our calling and God-sized miracles.

As we are right on the cusp of leaving the fourth stage, we'll prayerfully meet again in my next book so I can share the wisdom I'm excited to experience as I live in God's dream.

> Before I formed you in the womb I knew you,
> before you were born I set you apart (Jeremiah 1:5 NIV).

PART ONE:
The Two Great Encounters

Living in God's full purposes starts with two foundational Great Encounters:

1. **The First Great Encounter**: encountering Christ as our personal Lord and Savior

2. **The Second Great Encounter**: encountering God's revelation of His purpose(s) for our lives

CHAPTER ONE
The First Great Encounter: Cutting out Sin

To wait well, we all need what I'll call two great encounters. Our first "Great Encounter" is often referred to as the "ABC" of becoming a Christian: Admitting I am a sinner, Believing God sent Jesus to die and save me from my sins, and Confessing my faith in Jesus.

Having the saving knowledge of Jesus Christ is the first step we all need to wait well. Without Jesus as our foundation and cornerstone, we build in vain on sinking sand. This Great Encounter of salvation through Jesus is the life-changing one we wanted to shout from the rooftops when we first got saved.

Before I encountered Christ, waiting had no purpose. Waiting was shallow and tied to myself and personal gain. When set free, I wanted everyone to experience the joy and peace bestowed upon me. Not that everything was easy, because it wasn't. But I had a new found joy that wasn't tied to my circumstances once I received God's saving grace.

This Great Encounter must remain our anchor, foundation, and resting place during our waiting seasons. So let's park here just for a few moments.

Kudzu

Before moving to the south of the United States, I wasn't familiar with kudzu. Maybe you aren't either. We were taking a road trip from Tennessee to Florida. For miles, all the trees and vegetation were completely covered with lush foliage. To an ignorant eye like mine, it looked beautiful.

This stunning, lush foliage was actually kudzu, an invasive plant that kills trees by smothering and choking them. Be careful not to judge things by their beauty. It grows extremely fast, as much as a foot <u>a day</u>, even sixty feet during a season.

The kudzu canopy, while it may look beautiful, blocks the sun from providing the necessary nutrients to the trees underneath. It engulfs them and its weight alone can fracture or uproot an entire tree. The consequences to forestry in the southern United States is devastating.

In the same way, when sin starts out it usually looks so innocent and small. Just an innocent little phone call to a man or a woman who isn't our spouse, three months later can be a full-blown affair. Even if there's no consummated sexual activity, time spent in fantasy takes a heart away from where God intended. "Innocently" taking a ream of copy paper from work to use for our personal printer at home, after a twenty-year career equates to thousands of dollars worth of work office supplies stolen for our personal use (a pack of pens here, a ream of paper there, folders, labels, etc.).

Stepping into sin begins with small, seemingly harmless actions. But, just like kudzu, sin is invasive, it entangles us, and quickly spreads and grows. One day we wake up, look at our current reality and ask ourselves: "How did I get here?" We find ourselves engulfed in sin that's choking the life out of us. When looking in the mirror, we might not even recognize ourselves, much like those trees covered in kudzu.

The Bible says:

> And if you do not do well, sin is crouching at the
> door. Its desire is for you, but you must rule over
> it (Genesis 4:7 ESV).

> Then desire when it has conceived gives birth to
> sin, and sin when it is fully grown brings forth
> death (James 1:15 ESV).

After coming to Christ there was a six-year period where I remained sexually pure. I was determined to wait for my God-ordained husband. As a leader at my church, I taught purity at women's and youth retreats.

Yet, in transparent vulnerability, after six years of abstinence and strength, I rapidly found myself in a one-month toxic relationship. Almost instantly I was in the same predicament as years before.

Finally, devastated and overwhelmed, I scheduled a meeting with my pastor. I knew I had to confess but was fearful he'd remove me from leadership because of my lapse in judgment.

Yet, I knew I couldn't continue living a lie. My pastor asked for the man's name, asked for my phone and said, "Delete the file," as he permanently removed his contact information. Then my pastor said something so profound and redeeming that over a decade later I still remember as if it were yesterday: "I am going to tell you what Jesus told the woman at the well: 'Go and sin no more.'"

And just like that, he sent me on my way. I deserved instant removal from leadership but was extended grace. I never spoke to that man again.

Eight months later I met the love of my life, Emilio, who would become my husband nine months after our first encounter. Emilio is the Godliest and perfect man for me. Imagine if I had continued in that sinful relationship longer than that brief set back. I would've delayed meeting my husband and possibly even forfeited the best God had for me.

One thing I've learned about the enemy through my years of waiting is that he's patient. He'll devise schemes to harm us as a young child. It might take the form of an inappropriate touch, a rejection, feeling abandoned. If not healed, these hurts will inevitably impact future relationships.

Sufferings from long ago that take root sometimes don't manifest until ten, twenty or more years later. Remember, satan patiently perseveres. He knows his destiny and all he has is time, which we know from Revelation 12:12 is short.

What a glorious day when we first encounter our Savior, Jesus Christ! We come to Him weighed down and covered in kudzu, choking in sin. Then we encounter the truth of who we are, and surrender our lives to Jesus. He supernaturally removes the kudzu and allows us to walk in His forgiveness. Not that life becomes easy and we never sin again. But when we do fall short, there's a Savior who's waiting with open arms to guide and help us get back up.

Maybe today you're distressed and burdened with sin. You feel hopeless and are far from God or have never entered into a personal relationship with Jesus. I have great news! There's a way out. Reflect on these promises in scripture:

> If we confess our sins, he is faithful and just to forgive us our sins and to cleanse us from all unrighteousness (1 John 1:9 ESV).

> Therefore, if anyone is in Christ, he is a new
> creation. The old has passed away; behold the
> new has come (2 Corinthians 5:17 ESV).

We don't have to stay stuck. The process may not be easy and it'll take our complete surrender to God's perfect will, even when it hurts and even when we don't have all the answers. Whether "big" or "small," whatever the sin, it all separates us from God.

I use quotation marks because God doesn't put gradations on sin. A murderer is a sinner just like a petty thief who stole a pack of bubble gum. So today, no matter how far we are in this Christian journey, I suggest we pause right now and:

- Do a self-inventory
- Ask God to reveal our sins
- Ask Him to cleanse our hearts, and
- Repent and ask for help to resist the devil so he will flee.

We often hear people praying for revival, but revival starts with me. It starts with you. Pull back the kudzu and allow the S-O-N to shine down and provide the nutrients you need for eternal glory.

For seasoned Christians, the challenge is to not gloss over this chapter because our first "great encounter" of salvation was experienced years ago. A danger exists the more we believe none of these foundational truths apply to us as time moves us further from our glorious first encounter. I regularly remind myself: "when was the last time I really reflected on my salvation?"

God has new great encounters for us today, but maybe an invisible strain of kudzu is hiding the sunlight of the Holy

Spirit. Our sin may not feel as drastic or apparent as when we first encountered Christ. It's there nevertheless.

Taking the time in the beginning of our journey to do a self-inventory will probably reveal things in our lives needing to be cleared. Don't be surprised when God leads us to new, ever-deepening discoveries of freedom, even years after our first great encounter.

During the waiting period, there'll be many temptations to fall into sins because our enemy wants to keep us stuck in the waiting period so we delay or miss opportunities God has for us. Don't stay entangled in it. Cut it off.

CHAPTER TWO
The First Great Encounter: Learning from Snags

Snags

After the great encounter with our Savior Jesus Christ, something supernatural happens. God turns all these things that used to tie us down and cause so much agonizing pain, for good.

Wait, being sexually molested by my father was good? Abandoning my children and family for another relationship or alcoholism was good? No those things weren't good. But in God's hands, the turnaround can be used for His glory.

> And we know that *all things* work together for good to them that love God, to them who are the called according to his purpose (Romans 8:28 KJV, emphasis added).

"All things" means all things! God doesn't just use the good stories from our life. He miraculously uses all the messed up, painful details.

Continuing with the theme of forestry, let me introduce

the concept of snags, a critical part of ecosystems. I remember when my father retired and purchased six acres an hour outside of Chicago.

Previously, all we'd known was Chicago city living. As we walked through parts of the new property, we talked about needing to clear out all the dead branches, hollowed dead logs, and fallen trees in the forested areas.

Then I learned about the importance of snags. Snags are all the things I thought needed clearing: those same dead branches, hollowed logs, and fallen trees. It seemed like they were preventing other trees and plants from sprouting. But dead things serve a great purpose in God's ecosystems.

Species need snags to survive. Animals and insects borrow and find shelter in hollow logs. The dead wood provides necessary nutrients to the ecosystem as it decomposes. And these are just a few benefits. Additional facts exist for how nature uses death so life can continue.

Similarly, God has a way of using all those dead snags from our past to bring Him glory, especially those parts of our past that create the most shame. Someday, someone may be in a similar situation and we can help because we've overcome a similar shame, accepted God's forgiveness, healed, and moved on to higher ground. Our past may have been agonizing, but rest assured, God will use it, if entrusted to Him. God wastes nothing and is the best recycler.

There's a purpose in our pain. Our "snags" are the nutrients needed in bringing life to the ecosystem around us. There's power in the words of our testimony. "They triumphed over him by the blood of the Lamb and by the word of their testimony..." (Revelation 21:11 NIV).

Who is "him" that was triumphed over? The devil. So this scripture is telling us we triumph over satan through what Jesus did for us on the cross – "the blood of the Lamb" – and by those past snags God will use – the "words of our testimony."

Other translations for "triumphed" include: "defeated him," "conquered him," "overcome him," and "victorious."

In God's hands, our testimony is a gift, which has great power. He turns a test into a testimony and a mess into a message. The enemy's aware of this power and therefore tries to silence us in shame or fear to not share the words of our testimony.

When I was in sixth grade my parents went through a three-year, difficult divorce. I remember being removed from class in middle school to attend court hearings. I was torn between two parents and learned how to manipulate and harbored a lot of anger.

The divorce judge appointed me a guardian ad litem, who was an attorney to represent my best interest. I never remembered the name of the woman who was appointed, nor did I know she was an attorney. All I remember was she was the first person in the court system to listen and advocate for me.

These challenging experiences with a court advocate motivated me to attend law school so I, too, could help children in similar situations.

Years later, my father forwarded me an article asking: "Do you know who this is?" My sarcastic response read something like: "Someone who just got appointed to the Illinois Supreme Court?" Well, that same guardian ad litem who represented and motivated me to become an attorney, years later became a Supreme Court Justice.

Working in juvenile court I knew firsthand the often thankless job and few and far between success stories. I wrote a letter thanking her for the impact she had on my life, even though she may not remember me.

Much to my surprise, she hand wrote a letter back, describing how she remembered me and all the hardships I endured. She even asked to meet. We reconnected and years later she is still impacting my life.

As a result of this relationship birthed in the midst of one of my biggest crises, she was a keynote speaker at a gala for a non-profit I was leading. Her presence helped attract people to support the God work we were doing.

God used a very difficult time in my childhood to define the call on my life to become an attorney and child advocate. And years later, I also have an influential relationship with an amazing Supreme Court Justice. Not to mention all the other lessons I learned during the taxing divorce, like overcoming anger, hatred, and disappointment.

We never know how God is going to use our current pain for future blessing. It was not by chance that I'm able to uniquely relate to children whose parents are getting a divorce.

Waiting seasons are designed to heal from past hurts so our "snags" can be nutrients to help others. A holding pattern is a perfect time to release those unresolved hurts because there won't be room for them where God is taking us. Throughout our journey, we will explore practical ways to release them.

So God lifted the affliction of our sin, saved us from our sin, and then uses our past sin (or another's past sin inflicted upon us) for His glory! The miracle doesn't end there. God begins giving us Holy Spirit conviction, making us sensitive to sin, almost like being allergic to it. It's that inner voice telling us something isn't right.

And even when we fail to heed the warnings and start allowing some sin to grow, He always gives us an escape route to cut it from entangling us further.

No temptation has overtaken you that is not
common to man. God is faithful, and He will not
let you be tempted beyond your ability, but with
the temptation He will also provide the way of
escape, that you may be able to endure it (1
Corinthians 10:13 ESV, emphasis added).

During the one month of my unhealthy relationship
discussed previously, I made the choice to do the hard thing
and seek accountability from my pastor, even with the risk
of dire consequences.

Accountability and speaking the truth in love was my
"escape" First Corinthians 10:13 promised. Once I brought
my shame into the light, I was no longer living a secret and
felt a huge weight lifted. I escaped. If I'd continued, the
relationship would've entangled me further away from
God's perfect will for my life. Settling and compromises
always extend our waiting period.

Rear View Crash and Shoulder Bumps

On this same road trip in the southern United States, it was
my turn to drive. There was a semi-truck in front of me
going the same speed so I didn't need to pass. But it was
swerving back and forth all over the road, onto the shoulder,
then into the passing lane. I thought the driver was either
intoxicated or losing concentration from being on the road
too long. My instinct was to pass him because I didn't want
to be behind any potential accident.

It felt risky passing because I was worried he'd swerve
into the passing lane. When the opportunity came, I "put the
pedal to the metal," sped past him so he was in my rearview
mirror, and prayed for his and others' safety.

During our spiritual journey of waiting, God will give us

warning signs in front of us of an impending crash. Maybe it's a sexual relationship, a friendship riddled with flirtation, bad influence, addiction to social media filled with drama, pornography, cheating on our taxes, or any other temptation. It's visible through our front windshield of life with warnings and red flags.

We may try keeping our distance behind this temptation. But, just like this semi-truck, if we keep it in front of us, there's a huge risk of being caught in a crash (sin) that ultimately causes damage: spiritually, physically, emotionally, and perhaps financially.

While waiting, we have the opportunity to ask God what "intoxicated" things are in front of us, causing us to "swerve all over." He will warn of an imminent crash. He wants us to "put the pedal to the medal," speed past that semi-truck temptation, and escape the devastation that would inevitably play out in our lives. From our rearview mirror, it'll be called our past.

The process may feel scary and there may be a risk, like my fear of being removed from ministry leadership when confiding in my pastor about my sinful relationship. Don't be alarmed by fear. Use it to motivate you. Do it scared.

The enemy wants to use the potential consequences we fear to hinder our confession of whatever it is we're concealing. The devil knows when it's brought into the light we will be free. Let's remind ourselves of God's promises in First Corinthians 10:13.

He will always provide us with a way of escape. He'll give us a passing lane. The waiting period is designed to give us opportunities to act bravely in our confessions and learn how to be teachable.

Again, here's the danger: it doesn't matter how long we've been serving the Lord. Don't just skim past this truth with the same mindset that it doesn't apply because all those "hard" semis are already in our rearview mirrors. No one is exempt.

When I fell back into sin, I had six long strong years of purity. I was a leader in ministry. There were all kinds of warning signs the relationship was heading for a crash, and I was a seasoned Christian. As an attorney facilitating recovery programs, I've all too often seen the reality of people relapsing after years of sobriety.

I got arrogant in my sexual purity the more I traveled past the first semi and the further it was in my rear view mirror. And then, all of a sudden, I found myself in an unhealthy relationship which immediately landed me in the exact same place I was years before I encountered Christ.

Remember how fast sin grows? I'm so grateful my lapse in judgment only lasted a month because I sought the wisdom and accountability of my pastor.

Life's pauses are a great time to pass semi's.

CHAPTER THREE
The Second Great Encounter: Vision

Not only do we encounter Christ through salvation, but we also have another encounter when God gives us glimpses of His call and purposes for our lives. Let's call these glimpses the second "Great Encounter."

I remember clearly when and where my calling was first revealed. The revelation was a mere snippet and not the full picture. Yet, it was enough to catch and hold on to the vision.

Receiving God's Vision
Vision is so important for us and so important to God.

> "Where there is no vision, the people perish" (Proverbs 29:18 KJV).

If you haven't yet experienced this second "Great Encounter" or you aren't sure of the vision God has for your life, earnestly seek this revelation. Knowing God's specific purposes for our lives is imperative while waiting and preparing for them to manifest. If we don't know where we are going, there's a higher risk of giving up or wandering.

I've seen many struggle, not knowing their God-given purpose or dream. Some genuinely haven't received this revelation. However, I've witnessed some failing to recognize the vision God is trying to share because they were fearful or didn't like what they were being told, or it seemed so simple.

There are many reasons and ways individuals resist God's guidance.

Fight the urge to overcomplicate this great encounter with God's destiny. The experience may be an elaborate revelation or it could appear as something very straightforward. Rest assured, what appears ordinary will be larger than life when placed in the Master's hand.

My discovery was very simple and came in the form of a leader's conference. I was young in my career as a juvenile probation officer. My pastor brought me to an out-of-state leader's conference to catch the vision of their large bus ministry because my fiancé and I were leading our church's small bus ministry. Truthfully, ours was really a van ministry because we didn't own buses...yet.

I sat in a general session at the conference when the LA Dream Center came on stage and I saw former gang members, women who'd been prostituted, foster children, and other formerly broken individuals doing a step dance and worshiping God. I said to myself, "I have no idea what that is, but it's my calling."

No huge flashing lights or out of body experiences accompanied the epiphany. I didn't even fully understand it. At the time I thought I understood it, but through the waiting process, I learned I only knew a small piece of the puzzle that's still unfolding today. At inception, I simply knew, deep within my spirit that the call on my life was to help bring people who were marginalized, traumatized, rejected, and bruised to the feet of Jesus so they could walk in the fullness of all God purposed for them.

When this small view was exposed, I started with what I did know. I knew part of the call was at the grassroots level interacting one on one with hurting individuals. From the time I was a little girl, people have always opened up and shared their problems with me.

I often find myself meeting someone for the first time and, by the end of the interaction, having them confess things they've never told anyone. These experiences are always very humbling. It's surely nothing of my doing and is sometimes a huge responsibility to steward. It's truly a gift of God.

At the time of my second encounter, I also knew I was called to be a lawyer and top administrator in the largest juvenile court in the country. I've always had a unique God-given ability and gift to relate, interact, and inspire people from all different walks of life: those who were marginalized as well as those who had great power, wealth, and influence since I was born into a prominent physician's family.

I found myself in judges' chambers and with County Commissioners by day, and at night walking the streets of Chicago at 2:00 am ministering to women who were being prostituted and sometimes even their pimps.

Because these worlds are such polar opposites and I felt like I belonged in both, I remember going through an identity crisis early in this stage. I struggled knowing who I was because I loved and related to both. I even had a pastor tell me I had to choose and couldn't live in both worlds without being hypocritical.

Then right in the middle of this crisis, God used a total

stranger to speak a prophetic word. She approached me at a small church service in the presence of that same pastor who declared I had to choose.

Without any knowledge, this woman told me God was going to use me profoundly to be a "bridge" to get resources from people with great wealth and influence to impact people in poverty with little to no influence, all for the kingdom of God.

Twenty years into the journey, I've seen this word "bridge" manifest in so many ways and settings where God used this gift to connect totally different worlds. And I haven't even begun to witness it all yet. There's still so much more for God to reveal on my journey. I used the waiting period to work out these and many other insecurities.

God's call will inevitably evolve and expand as time passes and as we're given a clearer view of His bigger picture. At my initial revelation, I thought my calling was to help my church start and run a Dream Center in Chicago because we didn't yet have one.

However, there was so much more to my purpose than what I originally thought, which I will explain in more detail as we continue in our adventure together. The important point, for now, is I got a simple revelation, which quickened my Spirit, and I wrote it down and waited as clarity was revealed.

Inevitably, we will face discouragement. We may also believe we're doing something wrong. God will speak when we get into His presence and when we specifically ask for spiritual eyes to see, ears to hear, and a mind to discern His purposes for us. He doesn't withhold any good thing from His children (see Psalm 84:11). If we ask in His name, He is faithful to reveal His purposes and calling. And His timing is perfect.

A few things are for sure. Whatever your divine purpose is:

- It's bigger than you.
- It's not about you.
- It'll always have something to do with helping others and furthering the gospel.

In my experience, the purpose God gives is usually tied to the issues that bother us the most. The things that get under our skin and when we think about them, they bring us to tears. People can tell it's important from the tone of our voices and our body language. It's evident we have a passion to be involved as a catalyst for change.

Maybe it's the issue of abortion. Or, maybe, it's human trafficking, addiction, homelessness, education inequity, negative influences invading the creative arts, or elder abuse.

Remember, God may be trying to reveal His purpose, but we think it's too simple or ordinary, so we wait for more revelation. Yes, there may be more, but start with what is revealed and write that down.

> Do not despise these small beginnings, for the Lord rejoices to see the work begin, to see the plumb line in Zerubbabel's hand (Zechariah 4:10 NLT).

> If you are *faithful* in little things, you will be *faithful* in large ones. But if you are dishonest in little things, you won't be honest with greater responsibilities (Luke 16:10 NLT, emphasis added).

In Luke 16:10 the New International Version uses the

word "trusted" instead of the word "faithful" in both little and large things. God will usually give a little glimpse of His calling and we get to demonstrate faithfulness and trustworthiness in the little He reveals.

Be still and know that He is God (see Psalm 46:10). He will give us pieces to the full picture as we become ready.

Knowing God's dreams for our lives will be one of the keys to making it through the next stage in the journey: waiting and preparing for the dream to manifest.

Written Guarded Dreams

> And the LORD answered me: '*Write* the vision; make it *plain on tablets*, so he may run who reads it' (Habakkuk 2:2 ESV, emphasis added).

Once God reveals our calling, it's imperative to take some time the same day and write it down. Don't delay in this simple but critical task. It's biblical, as we read in Habakkuk 2:2. In addition, having the dream in written form has so many benefits, some of which are:

- It allows us to witness the expansion of our understanding as the years pass and more is revealed.
- It serves as a reminder of what God promised to keep us focused and not distracted or sidetracked by counterfeit plans.
- It helps get us through and anchors us to the truth when the inevitable difficult and challenging circumstances occur and we want to quit.

Dreams are meant to be written down, preserved, and guarded with discernment. Why guarded? Because not everyone can handle our God-sized dreams. A staff member on my team in ministry once told me these exact words: "You overwhelm me."

Her statement wasn't coming from a place of being overwhelmed with workload expectations. She was overwhelmed by the magnitude of the dreams birthing inside of me.

In our excitement, we must be careful who we let into our inner circles to coddle our God-given babies. We wouldn't entrust just anyone or a perfect stranger to watch our own children, would we? Of course not!

In the same way, we need to guard our dreams. There are dream killers and assassins who the enemy has deployed. And most come posing as "sheep." Those are individuals I call "sheep-wolves."

Don't get me wrong. Visionaries like me need people to rein us in and keep us grounded at times. But we have to be careful not to surround ourselves with people who are intimidated by and could assassinate the bigger-than-life God dreams inside of us. "*Beware* of false prophets who come *disguised* as harmless sheep but are really vicious wolves" (Matthew 7:15 NLT, emphasis added).

The New International Version says "Watch out for false prophets." Once we embrace God's dreams, "watch out" and "beware." Wolves will be "disguised" as sheep: sheep-wolves.

And we shouldn't be surprised when we're the only person who recognizes the sheep-wolf whom satan has sent to assassinate dreams. The scripture says the sheep-wolves will come "disguised," meaning they're not easily recognizable. I've seen them fool even the wisest of people.

We don't need to be paranoid, but discern and listen to God's voice and only entrust God's dreams to those with whom we have peace. This is especially necessary in the formative days of receiving our dreams when we are less confident in the assignment and more susceptible to debilitating insecurities. Opening ourselves up to the wrong people usually results in our insecurities being fed by their words and actions.

Nehemiah had a dream to re-build the walls of Jerusalem. He didn't go telling the whole world about what God told him to do. In fact, he only took a few people out to go inspect the walls and he went out at night:

> I went to Jerusalem, and after staying there three days I set out *during the night* with a *few others*. I had not told *anyone* what my God had put in my heart to do for Jerusalem. (Nehemiah 2:11 – 12 NIV, emphasis added).

In short, limit others access.

CHAPTER FOUR
The Second Great Encounter: Purposeful Design

Assigned in the Womb

Some common lies of the enemy while we wait are:

- God forgot about me or doesn't have a purpose for me because I'm just ordinary.
- It's too late to fulfill the purpose God has for me because I'm too old.
- I'm too far gone and have messed up too much for God to still have a purpose for my life.

These are all lies from the pit of hell. We received a God assignment before the womb. In the wise words of Les Brown in his book *Live Your Dreams*: "You are never too old to set another goal or dream a new dream."[2] If we still have breath in our lungs (even if we only have seven more days of life), live them with purpose.

> For you created my inmost being; you knit me together in my mother's womb. I praise you

because I am fearfully and wonderfully made;
your works are wonderful, I know that full well
(Psalm 139: 13-14 NIV).

Before I formed you in the womb I knew you,
before you were born I set you apart; I appointed
you as a prophet to the nations (Jeremiah 1:5
NIV).

These truths are so critical to waiting well for God's dreams to become a reality. During the lowest periods in my life, I learned to saturate myself and speak the truths in the word of God out loud. If you've never done this, go to the bathroom and speak the scriptures shared above and below out loud to yourself in the mirror.

I had scriptures posted all over my mirrors and house to directly attack my insecurities. They served as visual reminders everywhere I looked, so my mind remained steadfast on the word, leaving no space for distractions.

When I saw one, I'd speak it out loud into my life. An onlooker may have thought I was crazy talking to myself, but in my waiting years, I learned the power of the spoken word, even when I barely believed the truths I was declaring so vehemently.

With time, confessing them aloud, I began to slowly believe them. The bible says: "Death and life are in the power of the tongue, and those who love it will eat its fruits" (Proverbs 18:21 ESV).

Choose words wisely and make them obedient to what Jesus thinks of you. Not what others think, not what you think of your own self, and surely not what the enemy thinks of you.

So try it. In these next scriptures, I've changed the words

"we" and "you" to "I AM." Make this personal because YOU ARE chosen by God. Speak them out loud in front of a mirror over and over and don't be surprised if something inside breaks, as you begin to receive, believe, and embrace the truth.

> In him I am also chosen, having been predestined according to the plan of him who works out everything in conformity with the purpose of His will (see Ephesians 1:11 NIV).

> For I am God's masterpiece. He has created me anew in Christ Jesus, so I can do the good things He planned for me long ago" (see Ephesians 2:10 NLT).

> For he chose me in him before the creation of the world to be holy and blameless in his sight. In love He predestined me for adoption to sonship through Jesus Christ, in accordance with His pleasure and will (see Ephesians 1:4-5 NIV).

> But I am one of a chosen people, a royal priesthood, a holy nation, God's special possession, that I may declare the praises of him who called me out of darkness into His wonderful light (see 1 Peter 2:9 NIV).

> I did not choose God, but God chose me and appointed me so that I might go and bear fruit-fruit that will last-and so that whatever I ask in Jesus' name the Father will give me (see John 15:16 NIV).

> For I am a people holy to the LORD your God.
> The LORD my God has chosen me out of all the
> peoples on the face of the earth to be His people,
> His treasured possession (see Deuteronomy 7:6
> NIV).

> But I should always give thanks to God for you,
> brethren beloved by the Lord, because God has
> chosen me from the beginning for salvation
> through sanctification by the Spirit and faith in
> the truth (see 2 Thessalonians 2:13 NASB).

You are chosen. Let's act like it and ask God to reveal His purposes to us. In the meantime, look for additional life verses to combat any doubts trying to attack the truth about your purpose. Teach yourself and train your mind to not entertain such doubts by immediately combating them with the life verse you choose and commit to memory. You can train and condition your mind.

This exercise of repeatedly speaking a life verse may sound trivial – but don't be deceived. There is power in His word, for His word in your mouth is spirit and it is life (see John 6:63). His word never comes back void (see Isaiah 55:11 KJV). Self-affirmation through Christ is something so simple, yet so profound.

Orderly Seeds

While in a holding pattern we will also probably go through silent seasons where we feel alone. During those silent years, there's a temptation to think God's purposes are for everyone else but us. However, scriptures reveal we weren't placed on this earth randomly or by accident.

God's planting of us in an orderly way with specific

purposes reminds me of farmers' sowing patterns. When driving in the country have you seen those rows and rows of perfectly aligned crops zipping by? This pattern of perfectly aligned crops demonstrates the farmer's intentionality when planting seeds. He didn't merely throw them up in the air to land randomly. He methodically planted them in rows.

On a mission trip weeks before this book was published I was on an assignment with a retired farmer from Ohio. I shared with him this aspect of my book and without skipping a beat he rattled off how orderly seeds are when planted depending on the crop yielded.

I had to take out my phone to take notes and this is what he told me (he knew the same from memory for soy beans and much more): "Corn seeds are planted 6 inches apart and there are 32,000 seeds per acre or if planted 7 inches apart 27,500 per acre." I learned there is such specificity in how farmers place each seed. They know the exact seed count.

In the same way, the Lord didn't just throw us into this world without a specific purpose. God is a God of order. He placed us smack dab in the middle of our family for a purpose. He doesn't make mistakes. When He planted us as a seed in our families and in our marriages, He knew crops would be harvested through our births.

I have limited expertise in farming, but through all my observations, there's a lot of order and purpose in farmers' practices. Pause and read Isaiah 28:23-29 to see God's analogy through farming that exhibits beautifully and meticulously God's order and purpose. Verse 29 ends "All this [the description of farmer's activities] also comes from the Lord Almighty, whose plan is wonderful, whose wisdom is magnificent" (Isaiah 28:29 NIV).

We are God's wonderful and magnificent seed and He has an order and purpose for each of us. Hold on to that promise while waiting.

Relinquishing your Womb Assignment

Once we receive and accept the womb assignment and stop running, temptations to relinquish our calling appear while we are in holding patterns. When we watch a 3D movie and see the plot come together, do we turn to a perfect stranger next to us mid-movie and give them our 3D glasses? No. So, why do we give the assignment God has given us to someone else when we get impatient, fearful, or insecure?

The enemy tries to trap and derail us from pursuing God's assignments by making us think someone else will fill those shoes and fill them better than us. Yes, if we're disobedient, God can get someone else. But He really wants our obedience, so He can use our talents.

While waiting I actually walked away from an assignment God once gave me. Every year I led a mission team to the national football championship game to reach the thousands of individuals flown there to be trafficked. During the 2016 outreach, our team experienced a supernatural encounter where God showed me the darkness of where I was called to bring light. He revealed a specific assignment.

I've never experienced anything like the encounter I had in a hotel room during that mission trip. We were in San Francisco in 2016 and a huge trafficking ring formed at the hotel we were staying. I attempted to call in federal and local law enforcement, but they didn't respond.

After days of the ring growing, I gathered a group of prayer warriors inside a room to begin interceding. One of the women on the team was praying for each person in the room individually and when she got to me she stopped and we both fell to our knees first and then fell face down on the floor, cheek to cheek.

I felt a heaviness and weight on my back, suffocating the air out of me. I could barely breathe and the darkness all around me was overpowering. It felt like I was falling in a spiral into a black hole and there was torment all around me. I tried saying the name of Jesus and asked Him to bring the light and all I got out was a faint whimper. As I kept calling on His name, I felt relief and saw white lights flickering all around me.

After this intense intercession I asked each person in the room to describe what they saw. One of the volunteers said they saw the Arch Angel Michael touch my hips, which caused me to fall to my knees and then he was on top of me, hence the intense weight.

I knew then that God allowed me to experience and feel the torment and pain the women endure and it was my assignment to attend the championship game every year to be the light of Jesus and help bring them out of darkness. I share the full testimony in a book called "Voices Outside the Stadium"[1] in an encounter titled "Arch Angel Michael." This book is filled with encounters with trafficking victims at these annual major sporting events.

The very next year after this profound, defining, and confirming revelation, I found myself in a place where I wasn't able to attend the next outreach. In my absence, I handed everything over to a co-laborer who came for the first time the year before and she organized the team I'd been taking.

I was relinquishing the call God showed me by submitting to man who prohibited me from going. I didn't attend the outreach that year and cried the entire week of the game while the team conducted outreach to those being trafficked in my absence, despite the clear assignment from the year prior.

In 2018 I again found myself in a place where I wouldn't be attending and was feeling defeated and disobedient. But God intervened! Two months before the game, God brought a pastor into my life who asked me why I wasn't going. Without knowing the history, he looked at me and told me (as if he read my journal), "You need to be there." He wrote a check to make sure finances were not hindering me and I sat speechless with tears streaming down my face.

I attended the outreach and vowed, unless otherwise instructed by God, I'd never again miss the mission trip. The lesson? Stop trying to pass off what God has specifically assigned to us. God gave us an assignment and we need to be obedient to what He showed us.

Relinquishing assignments is nothing new. We're in good company. Sarai didn't trust in God's promise that Abraham would be the Father to all nations. Their circumstances didn't look like she could bear him children either and, instead of waiting and trusting in the promise, she got impatient and relinquished her rights to her Egyptian maid, Hagar.

She asked her husband to lay with this maid and marry her so she could have children through her. Hagar conceived a boy, Ishmael, causing jealousy and bitterness with Sarai whose name was later changed to Sarah.

Even though Sarah didn't wait, God remained faithful to His promise. When Sarah was beyond childbearing age, she bore a son Isaac, who fulfilled the promises of God. However, there were consequences to her disobedience that are still realized today.

Ishmael is the father of Islam, with both Christians and Muslims claiming rights to the Holy lands, one through Isaac and one through Ishmael, the son born as a result of trying to work things out in the flesh and not wait (see

Genesis 16, 17, 18, 21).

In the same way, relinquishing our assignment can have consequences that don't impact just ourselves but those we're supposed to reach out to. They hurt our legacy. I asked myself difficult questions to pinpoint why I relinquished this call on my life.

The answer to those questions was the root of rejection God wanted to dig up in my life, and I'm eternally grateful for His grace through the process.

As a side note, I also believe, once God revealed the call on my life, He took it away to see if I loved the "call" of ministry more than Him. Yes, ministry can become an idol. I am grateful for the year I relinquished my God-given assignment because it taught me how to sacrifice my gifts on the altar and give them back to God. I'm equally thankful that He allowed me to pick it up quickly, just as He gave Abraham and Sarah a second chance.

PART TWO: WAITING AND PREPARING

CHAPTER FIVE
Defining the War

Warrior in Training

Let's recap. God saved us, then He gave us a dream. He's revealed it to us and we've written it down. Great! Now get ready to wait. I can just see God in heaven whispering His plans in our ears, getting us all excited and pumped to jump, and then – of all things - Him casually pushing a huge pause button, and sitting back to relax.

For some, this isn't difficult because waiting comes naturally. That's my husband's DNA. He prays for something and poof, it happens! I believe God often answers his prayers expeditiously because he doesn't have a difficult time waiting.

For those like me, we pray, and ten years later God still has us waiting, trusting, and believing. That's why I've made Psalm 46:10 my life verse: I am still and know that He is God. My natural DNA loathes being still; hence the piece of the book title "I hate it." "Be still" is the life verse I often speak out loud to myself in the bathroom. Have you memorized your life verse yet?

Without the Holy Spirit, I'm terrible at waiting. I hate surprises. I want to know now and how. But God's normal pattern doesn't consist of giving me all the facts at once. And it's not because He's some cruel Father who gets a kick out of withholding information from me and watching me squirm.

The waiting is for my own good. I need it. In the waiting room, God built my faith muscles to trust in the unknown, the unseen, the supernatural, and the impossible. All the ingredients for this logical lawyer that aren't second nature!

God often doesn't reveal the whole picture because most of us couldn't handle the God-sized dream if it was exposed all at once. We'd get overwhelmed and perhaps crippled with fear because His dream for us is too big and too impossible. I am grateful for God's responses and promises when we get into overwhelming spaces:

> Jesus replied, 'What is impossible with man is possible with God' (Luke 18:27 NIV).

> No eye has seen, no ear has heard, and no mind has imagined what God has prepared for those who love him (1 Corinthians 2:9 NLT).

We know and quote these scriptures, but in practice do our thought patterns reveal we believe them? According to the second scripture, we have impaired eyesight, deaf spiritual ears, and are small minded. The waiting period is designed to open our eyes, ears, and hearts and nurture our belief in the impossible.

And that's not all. I believe God also holds back the entire picture from us because we would get in the way of it. If God had shown me the entire blueprint years ago at the leader's conference, I would've messed everything up. I would've formed committees and developed strategies for "how" God would use me to make it happen. And then when it came into fruition I would've tacked on "To God be the glory" when, in reality, God would not have had anything to do with it. I would've rushed ahead and tried to do it myself.

As you can see, I'm a logical person who likes to plan everything based on facts. Unfortunately, I prolonged the waiting periods ignoring this simple truth my pastor from Chicago often said to me, "Kaitrin, the "hows" are up to God. They aren't up to you." I'm forever grateful and indebted for God's patience with me.

Life's waiting rooms are also designed to teach us new ways to war and to build our character. "He *trains* my hands for battle; so that my arms can bend a bow of bronze" (Psalm 18:34 NASB, emphasis added). Like soldiers, we have to endure basic training that equips us for battle.

Think of it this way. While we wait God is fashioning us into a solid warrior with Godly character; a character that won't flinch under the disappointments, persecution, slander, oppression, difficulties, sicknesses, and hardships of all kinds that are bound to follow our God-given purposes. The waiting will toughen us up for the war tied to our destinies.

Defining the War

In order to comprehend the concept of spiritual warfare, it's imperative to acknowledge there's a war over our lives. Not that we are to give the enemy so much attention or go demon chasing.

But if we're in a war, it's important to know:

1. We're in a spiritual fight, and
2. The general nature of our enemy

As soon as we accept the call, we are sending out a signal declaring an all out war. When we had no concern about the will of God, we were not a threat. Now that we're serving God and wanting to reach the destiny He has for us, it shouldn't be surprising that we're going through unbearable trials.

In the wise words of one of my pastors, Pastor Efrain, whenever we're under attack, "consider it a badge of honor." We must be doing something right. The enemy is concerned and wants to distract, discourage, oppress, frustrate, and deceive us. And the closer we get to reaching God's destiny, the birth pains and warfare become harder and closer together. Anyone who's witnessed childbirth can recognize this truth.

Here are a few familiar scripture references depicting the spiritual war:

> For though we walk in the flesh, we are not waging *war* according to the flesh. For the weapons of our warfare are not of the flesh but have divine power to destroy strongholds. We destroy arguments and every lofty opinion raised against the knowledge of God, and take every thought captive to obey Christ (2 Corinthians 10:3-5 ESV, emphasis added).

> For we do not wrestle against flesh and blood, but against the rulers, against the authorities, against the cosmic powers over this present darkness, against the spiritual forces of evil in the heavenly places (Ephesians 6:12 ESV).

Now that we understand there's a war over our lives, it's also important to understand the nature of whom we're fighting in this war. Not that we spend an inordinate amount of time studying our enemy, but it's important to know his attributes so we can begin to recognize his schemes when he shows his face.

Our enemy is satan and his demons, what the bible sometimes refers to as "unclean spirits" (see Revelation 16:13 and Mark 3:11).

Here are a few of satan's attributes recorded in the bible: thief, deceiver, like a roaring lion (Jesus is the real Lion, satan is merely counterfeit), father of all lies, serpent, murderer (see John 8:44; 1 Peter 5:8; Revelation 20:10). Moreover, satan has rank in his camp. Ephesians 6:12 describes a hierarchy of rulers, authorities, and cosmic powers. Also study Matthew 12:43-45:

> Now when the unclean spirit goes out of a man, it passes through waterless places seeking rest, and does not find it. "Then it says, 'I will return to my house from which I came'; and when it comes, it finds it unoccupied, swept, and put in order. Then it goes and takes along with it seven other spirits *more wicked* than itself, and they go in and live there; and the last state of that man becomes worse than the first (NASB, emphasis added).

This clearly confirms some demons are "more wicked" than others.

The further we get into the war, the more we penetrate the enemy's camp. One of the purposes of the waiting period is for God to teach us to war at new levels.

Listen to the Apostle Paul's autobiography of his life after

He encountered Jesus on the road to Damascus. When he accepted his assignment (that included extensive travel, planting churches, and writing 8-13 books of the New Testament (depending on which scholars you ascribe some books to)), this was the cross he carried:

> Five times I received from the Jews thirty-nine *lashes*. Three times I was *beaten* with rods, once I was *stoned*, three times I was *shipwrecked*, a night and a day I have spent in the deep. I have been on frequent journeys, in *dangers* from rivers, *dangers* from robbers, *dangers* from my countrymen, *dangers* from the Gentiles, *dangers* in the city, *dangers* in the wilderness, *dangers* in the sea, *dangers* among false brethren; I have been in *labor* and *hardship*, through many sleepless nights, in *hunger* and *thirst*, often *without food*, in *cold* and *exposure*. Apart from such external things, there is the daily *pressure* on me of concern for all the churches (2 Corinthians 11:24-28 NASB, emphasis added).

Paul was lashed, beaten, stoned, shipwrecked, met dangers in all settings, labored, suffered hardships, sleepless nights, hunger, thirst, freezing cold, was naked, pressurized, and imprisoned (recorded in other epistles) during much of his Christian service.

Compare this with his lifestyle before following Christ, a life of power, prestige, and wealth. He traded all that for the cause of Christ and the physical suffering that accompanied warfare.

War isn't for the weak or fainthearted. You may look at Paul's character and feel discouraged because in comparison you don't feel like a tenacious warrior.

My brother, my sister, you are stronger than you think. Many great heroes of faith in the bible initially doubted their ability to accomplish great things for God, Moses and Gideon, to name only a few.

On our own we cannot accomplish great things. But in the perfect will of God, our dreams deposited from the Lord are possible, no matter what the attacks. The Word of God says:

> We are pressed on every side by troubles, but we are not crushed. We are perplexed, but not driven to despair. We are hunted down, but never abandoned by God. We get knocked down, but we are not destroyed (2 Corinthians 4:8-9 NLT).

Deep within each of us is a strong resolve for life and success. Stay focused. God asks us to surround ourselves with voices of faith during times of turmoil. Remain obedient. Push for greatness even when things don't make sense and we look mediocre. Let's make Jesus our anchor. Death could not hold Him. He's alive.

Power Embedded in Names

Rest assured, once we move forward into the things of God, the enemy knows our names. Don't be surprised, scared, or intimidated when he comes a-knocking.

Spoiler alert: we possess a fast-forward button and know the ending to the story. Satan's destiny is the lake of fire where he'll be tormented day and night, for eternity (see Revelation 20:10, 14–15).

We know wars have names: the Korean War, the Vietnam War, World War I and II, the Revolutionary War, the War on Terror. When we mention the name of these wars to someone who lived through or fought in them, all kinds of emotions are stirred up.

Power is embedded in a name. Well, guess what? There is a name for your war too! Is your name Sarah? There is a Sarah War. Is your name James? There is a James War. Your name is prophetic.

In my experience, our wars and struggles are commonly linked to the meaning of our names.

Let me explain: my name Kaitrin means purity. But remaining pure was my struggle before encountering Christ. Then there was Jennifer, a woman in one of our addiction recovery programs. Jennifer never felt pretty or good enough, leading her to define her self-worth in men. Do you know her name means "Fair Lady"?

Mary, another woman in the program, held on to hurts and didn't listen to that "inner voice" when danger was lurking, which often landed her in compromising positions. Her name means "bitter and rebellious." Regina, whose name means "Queen" always settled for less than her royal status.

Tears of joy well up as I reflect on God's faithfulness to you Jen, Mary, and Regina. Each graduated the program and is living a purpose-driven life, to the glory of God!

Every week in the recovery program I taught on spiritual warfare. For three years, I'd teach a class when women first arrived in the program before I knew their specific struggles. I researched the meaning of each woman's name and prayed for a prophetic word in how their name was associated with their lifelong struggle.

Every time, without fail, God penetrated hearts and revealed truths. Self-awareness of their true identity began healing concealed scars.

During our waiting season, we need to date ourselves to learn and know our weaknesses. The enemy knows our name and the purposes God assigned to us. And so does God. Remember, God knit us together in our mother's womb and calls us by name. When we accepted Jesus our name got written into the book of life (see Revelation 20:15). God knows and God counted every hair on our head (see Luke 12:7; Matthew 10:30).

Research the meaning of your name (if you don't already know it) and ask God to reveal how the enemy has attacked God's divine purposes on your life as expressed by your name.

If you've changed your name, look up your original birth name and also ponder the meaning of that name. If you don't see a link, feel free to send me a message on my website: kaitrinvalencia.com. I'd love to share insight.

CHAPTER SIX
Battle Perspective

Finding our Battle Cry

In past wars, there was something known as a battle cry. These were the words and slogans soldiers shouted out in solidarity as they advanced toward their enemy. Instruments such as trumpets were also blown to intimidate the enemy.

When we're under attack, what's our response? What battle cry do we let out so our enemy can hear? If I'm honest, my natural responses when under attack are panic, fear, doubt, retreat, isolation, intimidation, and defeat.

When I began moving forward and taking huge leaps of faith, my family came under extreme attack, specifically in our health and finances. Once my nine-year-old daughter got an infection above her eye, causing her entire face to swell. I slept for three days in her bed, waking at her every breath and turn.

Initially, I was scared and downcast because the infection got worse as the days progressed. I took her to urgent care and they said it was viral and could, therefore, not prescribe anything. When the swelling spread overnight down her face, I took her to the emergency room. There they diagnosed her with a serious staph infection and finally gave her antibiotics.

I took pictures every day to compare the swelling. After a day of antibiotics, the swelling still got worse and continued to advance. My physician father was gravely concerned and advised me to go to the emergency room.

I stayed up until two in the morning and warred and prayed over our baby girl; yet it got progressively worse. I felt helpless, discouraged, and defeated. Minute by minute, I made God smaller and my mountain bigger.

Then my husband (as my accountability partner and encourager) reminded me that the enemy needed to hear worship come out of my mouth, no matter what was happening in the natural. Shifting my perspective to God's, my battle cry began to rise in warfare, no matter what my physical eyes were seeing.

My battle cry became praise, for praise rising out of God's people is warfare (see Psalm 75; Psalm 149). My perspective shifted and within days of worship, the infection began pouring out of the sore and she was healed. Glory to God!

All too often I see people burdened with grief over personal matters or attacks in their world. It's during those times we need to remind ourselves that the burden is not ours to carry. Surrender it to Jesus and trust He is fighting our battle. Sound the trumpet and watch God move. It can be so hard, but when we truly surrender and lay it down, an indescribable peace will come upon us. Even when it doesn't make sense and even when God doesn't respond the way we ask.

The Shofar

The shofar is an ancient trumpet used for a battle cry in biblical times. It's is a ram's horn with great meaning in Israel and is used during Jewish festivals and holidays. The variations in the blowing of the horn developed different meanings through time. One of the calls, the t'ruah, is nine quick bursts, which alerted Israel that they were under attack. The t'ruah was the sound prompting them to rally for battle. It was the battle cry.

For those who've never heard the sound of a shofar, I encourage listening online. Better still, get your own shofar and sound it as strategic times in your own battle ground. When I hear the sound, it penetrates to my bones.

So I ask today: what's in your lungs, your human breath or the breath of God? It can only signal one of two things: defeat or a battle cry. The walls of Jericho fell at the long blast of the shofar and a collective shout (see Joshua 6:5).

Anything less than blowing the shofar in a forceful breath to tell the enemy we're ready for battle is defeat. Sound the shofar battle cry today as a sign to your enemy that power and victory are in your lungs.

No matter the magnitude of the enemy or size of the mountain facing us, be equipped with God's perspective. Just as we wouldn't relinquish our 3D glasses to someone else, neither would we watch the 3D movie with glasses on our lap. Without the 3D glasses on, we wouldn't get the right perspective and everything would be hazy.

In the same way, when we gaze at our battle through our natural eyes, we'll have the wrong perspective. We must learn to filter our vision through God's 3D glasses to experience the plot through the Creator's battle plan.

What perspective should we have for battle? How about these two?

When you go to war against your enemies and see horses and chariots and an army greater than yours, do not be afraid of them, because the Lord your God who brought you up out of Egypt, will be with you. When you are about to go into battle, the priest shall come forward and address the army. He shall say: 'Hear, Israel: Today you are going into battle against your enemies. Do not be fainthearted or afraid; do not panic or be terrified by them. For the Lord your God is the one who goes with you to fight for you against your enemies to give you victory' (Deuteronomy 20:1-4 NIV).

This is what the Lord says to you, 'Do not be afraid or discouraged because of this vast army. For the battle is not yours, but God's. Tomorrow march down against them...you will not have to fight this battle. Take up your positions; stand firm and see the deliverance the Lord will give you...Do not be afraid; do not be discouraged. Go out face them tomorrow, and the Lord will be with you...As they began to *sing and praise*, the Lord set ambushes against the men of Ammon and Moab and Mount Seir who were invading Judah, and they were defeated (2 Chronicles 20: 15-16, 17, 22 NIV," emphasis added).

In the natural, the Israelites were defeated because there was no way they could escape from the armies closing in on them. But, on hearing from the Lord and executing His plan, they commissioned their strongest forces to lead the charge. Who were they? The singers and dancers, praising the Lord!

And a supernatural thing happened. The enemy armies were thrown into confusion and began fighting among themselves so much so there were none left alive. And when the Israelites came to take away the valuable plunder, it took three days (see 2 Chronicles 20:22-25). Three days for an entire army!

We've all faced battles and tried to fight them in our own strength and strategies. During the waiting and preparation stage, God will teach us to surrender our battles to Him and avoid the wrong plan of action by fighting on our own.

As these scriptures reveal, the battle isn't ours. It belongs to the Lord and when we submit the war outcome to Him, He has the victory. The victory may not come packaged the way we envisioned it because our ways are not His ways (see Isaiah 55:8).

Listen to Michael W. Smith's song, *"Surrounded (Fight My Battles)"*[3] to reinforce God's battle perspective. And remember, when you surrender the battle to the Lord, resist the temptation to pick it back up.

We went through a very difficult time at our church with one of our close friends and leaders in ministry fighting cancer. She and her husband had tried for years to conceive a baby and finally won the war of infertility and birthed a beautiful girl. When their daughter was small we got the news of her mom's fight with this aggressive form of cancer, and within a year she went to be with the Lord.

During her cancer battle, there were thousands of people warring and crying out to God. While it may appear we were defeated when she went to be with the Lord, God had the final say. He could've instantly healed her but in His infinite wisdom, He brought her home.

Yes, there were moments of questioning and asking God, "Why?" These sentiments still creep in even now. Why would He have them wait so long to conceive, finally answer their prayers, just to have her pass away a few short years later?

In the midst of the pain and loss, we pushed through this tragedy and witnessed our friend's legacy impact so many. It hasn't been easy, but I have seen her widowed husband, daughter, siblings, parents and friends press into God in unprecedented ways.

Years later, her widowed husband, who was devastated beyond words, met and wed a godly woman with no children. I've watched God use her to fill a void that every girl needs – a maternal figure. No, she will never replace her biological mother (who is with our heavenly Father), but she will be used as a surrogate mother and she loves her like her own. Love and miss you, Niome!

I truly believe that because our widowed friend battled (even when it hurt, even when it didn't make sense, and even when he may have been angry at God) that God heard his cry and blessed him with a beautiful, God-fearing second wife.

Read Romans 8:11 and listen to Jeremy Camp's song *"Same Power."*[4] We have the same power living inside us that rose Jesus from the grave. Let's resolve in our spirits to let this be a year of strength for us and our family, no matter what wars we may face.

I believe we're living in a time where God is mobilizing people who will push through fear and hesitation, people who will tap into the same power that rose Jesus from the dead, as we boldly tell satan – CHECKMATE! Which means, as an army of ambassadors for Christ, there is nowhere for satan to go. In this chess game of life, he has no moves left; he's cornered. He's defeated. We have the victory. Niome and all those who died in Christ are victorious in heaven, with no more pain and a great legacy.

Is this your battle perspective today? That you have the blood of Jesus pumping through your veins? Say with me: "I choose to keep moving forward into the enemy's camp and not let satan or any demon in hell cripple or paralyze me any longer."

Don't be intimidated, retreat, or look back to the wilderness when facing giants in your advance. Focus ahead on the destiny God has and watch Him fight the battles, even when others are shrinking back in fear and even when things don't make sense or hurt. And when you inevitably have a bad day warring, get up the next day, put on your full armor, and reclaim lost ground.

Maybe you look at yourself and think, "I'm an unlikely candidate." Others may have the posture or disposition of the warrior hero, but not you. You may feel timid, quiet, a follower, not a leader, or insecure.

I have great news. God isn't looking at our outward appearance, He's looking at our inward warrior spirit that's rising up during our waiting period. First Samuel 16:17 says:

> But the Lord said to Samuel, 'Do not look on his
> appearance or on the height of his stature,
> because I have rejected him. For the Lord sees not
> as man sees: man looks on the outward
> appearance, but the Lord looks on the heart' (1
> Samuel 16:7 ESV).

In the waiting war, possess the right battle mind and learn a battle cry so the enemy hears and retreats.

CHAPTER SEVEN
Childlike Faith

Truly, I say to you, unless you turn and *become
like children*, you will never enter the kingdom of
heaven (Matthew 18:3 BSB, emphasis added).

My husband and I had encountered no major changes in our
ten years of marriage up to then: same jobs, same house,
same church, and same schools for our kids. Suddenly, we
were thrust into a season of great decision-making and life-
altering transitions. After much prayer and deliberation, we
decided I would leave my job with juvenile court and move
into full-time ministry.

Then, around two and a half years into this huge
transition, we found ourselves interviewing for a ministry
job in another state ten hours away and asking God for His
direction.

One day we prayed and good "Christianese" prayers
came out of my mouth. "God give us wisdom as we make
decisions. Guide us. May there be clarity in what you want
us to do. Open doors and close doors. Give us courage and a

childlike faith.....”

Bam! My husband instantly dropped my hands mid-prayer and asked sternly, "WHAT ARE YOU DOING?"

I was dumbfounded. "I was praying," I responded. Duh! I thought, "how rude to interrupt my Holy Spirit inspired prayer!"

He responded: "Do you know what you just prayed for?"

Simply put, I didn't even realize. Words were just coming out of my mouth, almost like scripted prayers. There's a saying you've probably heard or even said yourself: "Be careful what you pray for."

Well, my spirit knew what I needed. I innocently prayed for a "childlike faith" and God, in His faithfulness and loving kindness, granted my prayer. My next season was filled with ample opportunities for my forty-two year old self to exercise childlike faith. and battle perspectives like my then 10, 8, and 5-year-old children.

We took the job in faith ten hours away and went from owning a house to renting an apartment, while we waited for our house a few states away to sell. While the sale took almost one year, our five-year-old child was clueless.

He didn't worry about how the lights would remain on and how food would keep being served. He kept asking: "How much longer are we staying at this hotel?" This was his pure "childlike faith" battle perspective.

In the natural, our Chicago house and utilities were $2,000 monthly and our rent in Memphis was $1,350 plus utilities with income that wouldn't sustain this much in housing. Every month we trusted. And every month, guess what? Yes, God provided just enough. He supernaturally provided the precise amount we needed to get through each month.

I'd always heard testimonies from missionaries and people in full-time ministry who shared this type of experience. But to live through one personally? It was a wrenching season of stretching.

Sounds great and like the God we all know, right? Well, this was an unfamiliar stretching and dependence for me. I grew up a very privileged child. I went to a great suburban High School, had a car when I turned of age, went to all the summer camps (that now as a parent I know cost thousands of dollars), went on lavish vacations (some even overseas) with great hotels and lobster dinners. I never once even thought about a meal being provided for breakfast, lunch, and dinner.

My husband, on the other hand, grew up poor and depending on God in extraordinary ways. His parents emigrated from Mexico when he was young. Both parents worked very strenuous jobs to provide for their six children, often standing in line at food banks. He grew up experiencing God as Provider on a whole different level.

So when I prayed a "childlike faith" prayer, he knew what would follow. He was familiar with the required battle cry. Years after this prayer of mine, when we were living for months on one income, my husband would ask: "Have you told God you learned your lesson and don't need any more childlike faith lessons? You asked for this."

In retrospect, I wouldn't change my drastic prayer made in ignorance. What followed was difficult, but I needed those childlike faith lessons to learn a new battle cry.

Imagine if we all prayed those dangerous radical prayers. They'd stretch us beyond the borders of our comfort zones. Prayers for patience could set into motion every irritating and frustrating thing to teach us that lesson. These life-defining prayers, while challenging, catapult us to experience supernatural growth. We experience unprecedented opportunities to witness God's hand and experience His miracles and tangible love specific just for us. It's where a line is drawn, separating the natural from the supernatural.

When we step into this realm, two key elements are essential no matter what storm hits: obedience and praise. We will go through the fire – as the bible promises. When the fire hits the highest point, do we back away in disobedient retreat? Or do we trade in praise for complaints, doubt, or anxiety.

Waiting well means we live in obedience and wear a garment of praise, no matter the cost. Only then do we exit the fire as refined precious gold.

> Behold, I have refined you, but not as silver; I have tried you in the furnace of affliction (Isaiah 48:10 ESV).

After enduring our lowest point financially when I was unemployed for 10 months, I remember bouts of feeling sorry for myself, complaining, and questioning God. Many days I lay flat on my face crying for hours in God's presence singing a new sonnet. It was during that time He broke something so deep inside, causing a supernatural peace and reliance on Him.

> To appoint unto them that mourn in Zion, to give unto them beauty for ashes, the oil of joy for mourning, the *garment of praise* for the spirit of heaviness; that they might be called trees of righteousness, the planting of the Lord, that he might be glorified (Isaiah 61:3 KJV, emphasis added).

A year later I found myself restored as a result of my

obedience to not give up and my relentless "garment of praise." I remember the next winter starting our day off by waking up in a freezing cold house we purchased less than 30 days earlier.

Later in the day, we learned our two furnaces needed to be replaced. My husband left for work that morning and in the middle of the expressway, his engine cracked beyond repair. And, lastly, my refrigerator broke and began leaking water inside. So in one day two furnaces broke to the tune of over $9,000, we needed a new vehicle engine estimated at over $2,000, and our fridge was broken.

What did I do? The old me would've panicked and complained in frustration. The new refined me cranked up praise music in my space heater warmed room and danced in worship, which resulted in laughing so hard at the devil. Sometimes when all hell breaks out, all we can do is laugh. It's good medicine (see Proverbs 17:22).

We have a tendency to look at others and want the anointing, the favor, and blessings. But we don't want the process. We do not see the warfare attached to the person who finally won.

> And I will put this third into the fire, and refine them as one refines silver, and test them as gold is tested. They will call upon my name, and I will answer them. I will say, 'They are my people'; and they will say, 'The Lord is my God' (Zechariah 13:9 ESV).

> So that the tested genuineness of your faith – more precious than gold that perishes though it is tested by fire – may be found to result in praise and glory and honor at the revelation of Jesus

Christ (1 Peter 1:7 ESV).

During the year we waited for our house to sell hundreds of miles away and paid insurmountable housing costs in two states. I learned about God's dew and daily manna from heaven. He fed us and provided for our every need.

> For there will be peace for the seed: the vine will yield its fruit, the land will yield its produce and the heavens will give their *dew*; and I will cause the remnant of this people to inherit all these things (Zechariah 8:12 NASB, emphasis added).

The mounting financial burdens culminated in both my husband and me losing our jobs simultaneously. In an instant, we went from being the people who generously gave to those going through hardship, to being the one who didn't know how we were going to pay our light bill or rent.

But against that sea of expenses, God remained faithful for ten unemployed months. Someone wrote a $1,000 check during a meeting at Starbucks to cover the fees I needed to apply to practice law in the state to which we relocated.

Another time a family sowed a $500 check coming out of a Wednesday night service. Earlier that week I had tears streaming down my face, crying out to God, not knowing how we were going to pay our almost $500 gas, light, and water bill. And these are just a few examples of literal manna provided for our family.

Hearing these testimonies from others was amazing, but to live it myself took humility. When the manna first started falling, in all honesty, I felt like a charity case. I was embarrassed to be on the receiving end and didn't want to receive what I felt was a handout.

Yet these lies were far from the truth. People genuinely

loved us. They wanted to help and we did not even ask or make known our needs. We prayed. God spoke to people and they responded in obedience.

God showed me in the waiting season that I was really good at giving but was terrible at receiving. To make it worse, He specifically showed me it was a form of arrogance and pride. I was prideful to think I didn't need help and to turn help away. God chiseled the pride away and allowed me to let others help and love me in the midst of our difficulty.

While waiting, be open to enjoy and feast on God's manna.

CHAPTER EIGHT
Weapons of Mass Destruction

Great! I need to go to war and have the right battle perspective and pray crazy, fanatic prayers. But how exactly do we war once the fire hits? These are the ways I've learned:

1. Prayer/Intercession
2. Reading, praying, speaking, and writing God's Word
3. Fasting
4. Keeping accountable and not isolated
5. Obedience to God
6. Love and honor
7. Repentance
8. Forgiveness
9. Humility
10. Praise, worship, and thanksgiving
11. Generosity
12. Persistence – not giving up

When we engage, model, and embrace these, we're fighting the enemy and putting a stake in the ground to reclaim territory he stole.

The famous warfare verse in the bible is Ephesians 6:10 where we're taught how to "put on the full armor of God." We're saved by grace but we're not automatically dressed in armor. We have to take action and "put on" God's armor.

We wouldn't go somewhere knowing we were going to engage in something physical and wear high heels, right? Of course not! Especially not a man! We must take time and put on the proper fighting gear for war.

Are we living defeated because we're showing up to battle with the wrong armor or worse, no armor at all? The women in our recovery program were taught to recite Ephesians 6:10 from memory as a group every morning. Have you put on your armor today?

Have you fastened all the buckles on your "belt of truth" (v. 14)? Or are you walking around exposed, with your pants down, because you believe the enemy's lies whispered in your ears? Did you leave your "shield of faith" by your bedside this morning, so when you learn of disturbing news today you're distraught with fear and anxiety?

The commandment is to put on the "full" armor, not some armor. Otherwise, we will be exposed and unprotected in areas we fail to protect. Notice our back is the only unprotected area in God's armor. Why is this important? Because we cannot show our backs to our enemy and run, expecting to win. We must always face our enemy and not hide or run. Stand your ground. No retreating.

Power Generator
A central part of our full armor can be found in verse 18:

"And pray in the *Spirit* on all occasions with all kinds of prayers and requests." My prayer is for us to experience supernatural warfare to overcome obstacles and loneliness, fear, doubt, and insecurity through the power of the Holy Spirit. We need the power of the Holy Spirit to show us how to war.

> But you will receive power when the Holy Spirit comes on you; and you will be my witnesses in Jerusalem, and in all Judea and Samaria, and to the ends of the earth (Acts 1:8 NIV).

The Holy Spirit isn't something only experienced on the day of Pentecost. The Holy Spirit is not just there to comfort and teach us but to give us blueprints for war.

Anyone who's taken a road trip across the United States has witnessed fields of the white three-pronged windmills rotating throughout the horizon. One day we pulled into a gas station and an extremely long semi-truck was carrying just one of these windmill blades.

My family walked over to inspect it. To describe this blade as enormous is an understatement. As I stood next to it, I wondered how something so massive and so heavy could be moved by slight amounts of wind to produce energy. It defied logic.

According to the National Wind Watch, the most widely used windmill blade is 116 feet, weighing about 14,000 lbs, and is placed on top of a 212-foot tower. The blades have vertical airspace of almost one acre.

Logically speaking, the windmill blade is too heavy and large to be moved by a slight wind. In order for these massive blades to move with the wind, they must be manufactured by an engineer and craftsman with specific angles and shapes to produce an uneven pressure that captures the wind's energy, which causes the blade to spin. In this way the wind can be harnessed to create energy for 750 U.S. homes in one year.

Great! So what does any of this engineering lesson have to do with waiting, the Holy Spirit, and warfare?

Today you may see obstacles or things in your life that feel too heavy to move, like those 14,000 lb blades. Or maybe you're facing situations that feel impossible. Maybe you're avoiding a mountain that God wants you to face, so He can supernaturally move it. A sickness? A failing marriage? A wayward child? A loss of employment? Insurmountable debt?

Consider this: the Holy Spirit is characterized in scripture with wind and breath (see Acts 2:2; John 20:22; John 3:6-8). "And suddenly there came from heaven a noise like a violent rushing *wind*, and it filled the whole house where they were sitting" (Acts 2:2 ESV, emphasis added).

Can we press into our engineer and craftsman God, who created us as a masterpiece? When we do, He'll harness the wind of the Holy Spirit to supernaturally move what feels too big, too impossible (massive windmill blade), and produce enough energy (faith) – not just for ourselves, but for all those around us (those 750 homes).

When Jesus left, He said He was leaving us a Comforter, the Holy Spirit. Let's allow the Holy Spirit wind to be our power generator today so we can soar beyond logic and our limitations into all the miracles He has for us.

I would never have believed the wind could move those huge blades until I saw hundreds of them working in action. In the same way, God will allow us to see and experience His miracles when we learn how to harness the Holy Spirit's power which God has specifically fashioned for us to experience.

Don't quench the Holy Spirit or be afraid to tap into His power. It's readily available to every believer. I'd rather be called one of those "weird Christians" than deny the power of the Holy Spirit. I've unfortunately seen movements that attempted to water down the gospel by quenching the power, the presence, and the manifestation of the Holy Spirit.

Unfortunately, we've become a society that is afraid of offending or making people feel uncomfortable. We've become accustomed to putting on our politically correct smile and mouthing the platitudes of the day. So many are putting the Holy Spirit in their own tidy man-made boxes to make people feel "comfortable."

Listen, the Holy Spirit is a Person whom man cannot control. The Holy Spirit doesn't operate in our man-made constraints and timers. Yes, God is a God of order. His order is for Him to be the One in control of all we say and all we do, period.

The Holy Spirit is one of the most powerful weapons of mass destruction. While waiting, tap in and learn to receive the power God gives to each follower of Jesus Christ through the Holy Spirit.

War with Words We Speak

Another weapon of mass destruction is the power of your spoken words. We learned from scripture how words have the power of "life and death."

When I was taking the bar exam, all kinds of thoughts and insecurities swarmed my mind which sounded something like this:

- "I spent over $100,000 on an education and if I don't

pass this one test, I'll never be an attorney."
- "I'm not smart enough to pass this test."
- "There's too much material to learn and memorize" (as I sat and looked at endless stacks of books)."

One day in the midst of my mind spiraling into an abyss of self-doubt, I stood up with an attitude and boldly screamed: "No, I cannot do this! And yes, I'm not smart enough! And, yes, it's impossible to memorize and learn all this material! But even though I cannot do this, I CAN do ALL things through Christ Jesus who gives me strength" (quoting Philippians 4:13 BSB). Remember, even if you don't believe the truths you're speaking out loud, speak them anyway.

One day I was praying out loud these words in my car: "Satan, my mind is not your playpen, for you to cage me in and play with my thoughts, attitudes, and beliefs." I pulled over and started reflecting on my prayer and this is what the Holy Spirit gave to me.

"When I was a child, I spoke and thought and reasoned as a child. But when I grew up, I put away childish things" (1 Corinthians 13:11 NLT). I'm not a child. I'm a grown woman. I don't belong in a baby playpen.

Be encouraged today to declare and tell the enemy that your mind is not his playpen. As believers of the Most High God, we must stop having a "playpen" mentality when we're called to be free, not restricted.

During the season of taking the bar exam and feeling defeated and incapable, the Philippians 4:13 scripture became my life verse.

I know I keep asking, but it's key: have you memorized your life verse yet?

Whenever those negative, lying, defeating thoughts came

to mind during my studies, I spoke that life verse out loud to myself. I would take captive the thoughts before insecurities flooded my mind and spiraled out of control. I spoke the truth I had memorized from the word of God (see 2 Corinthians 10:5 NIV). I refused to confine myself to the playpen the enemy had designed to keep me confined.

For those like me, it's a constant battle to make sure truth is spoken out of our mouths. In the journey of writing this book, I battled with feeling that everything I wrote was so "basic" and I had nothing new to say. I had my closest friends read drafts and was incredibly intimidated at the prospect of sharing what I labored over for countless hours. What if it was terrible? What if it was boring?

In the middle of the process, I made some of these comments to my husband, specifically the insecurity of the book feeling so "basic." His immediate words after reading twenty pages were a rebuke spoken in love: "Let that be the last time those words come out of your mouth." Nothing inspired by God is basic.

> The tongue has the power of life and death, and those who love it will eat its fruit (Proverbs 18:21 NIV).

> Don't use foul or abusive language. Let everything you say be good and helpful, so that your words will be an encouragement to those who hear them (Ephesians 4:29 NLT).

In the midst of this instability, I found myself in everyday conversations speaking about a principle I wrote in this book the previous day. And, it would bless someone. I believe these confirming conversations were God's gentle way of continuing to nudge me forward into my destiny, despite insecurities, assassins, and sheep-wolves.

Pause and listen to TobyMac's song *"Speak Life."*[5] It's a great illustration of the power of words we speak. We have enough strife, anger, and division in our world. Today, I choose to use my words to speak life and encouragement to those in my sphere of influence, including to myself.

CHAPTER NINE
Warring to Maturity

When we begin using all the weapons of mass destruction and engage in warfare it'll most likely feel foreign. Many, if not all, can relate to the insecurity felt the first time you prayed out loud.

I remember the first time I was asked to use one of my weapons of mass destruction and pray in public, I was mortified. I'd just experienced the first great encounter we discussed and, while I loved attending church services, smaller bible studies before services were intimidating. This small group setting didn't feel safe because I knew very little about the bible. Everyone was knowledgeable and prayed confidently and eloquently.

In service, there was a safe one-way conversation with the Pastor speaking from a pulpit and me absorbing every nugget of wisdom sitting in my pew. No threats existed where I'd have to say or know something. In these bible studies, people were participating, sharing and corporately praying. I was okay being the quiet one. Strange for a lawyer who in most situations had something to say! However, these small groups didn't lend to hiding easily.

After years of God depositing truths in me about Himself and who He created me to be, I now have confidence to come boldly to the throne of grace. After much preparation and waiting God has transformed me into a formidable enemy of the adversary. I am no longer timid but reliant upon the indwelling power of the Holy Spirit to intercede.

The more time we spend with someone in their presence, the more comfortable we feel being ourselves and speaking earnestly to them. I had to learn, through practice and seeing with my own eyes, the power of spending time with my heavenly Father in warfare through prayer. "The prayers of the righteous person is both powerful and effective" (James 5:16 NIV).

When I was asked to pray for the first time out loud, I was a baby drinking milk, and not a mature Christian eating solid food. The more obedience I practiced and the closer I got to reaching God's purposes for my life, the more intense the warfare. When I was serving in ministry at level 3, I encountered warfare at level 3. When serving in ministry at level 8, I was seeing and experiencing warfare at level 8.

Not that the enemy's soldiers weren't in the room when I was serving at level 3. But I wasn't the threat then that I am now. The moment I took a step of faith closer to God's purposes, I activated another level of the enemy's schemes that required intensified warfare. And the more mature and skilled I became in warfare, the more discernment I've needed to recognize good and evil.

Unfortunately, I've seen the concept of new levels, new demons hinder many of God's children from taking the next leap of faith. I remember not wanting to immerse myself completely in God's plans because it meant heightened susceptibility to attacks on my family. This fear was not a spirit God gave me. "For God hath not given us a spirit of fear; but of power, and of love, and of a sound-mind" (2 Timothy 1:7 KJV).

I pray we don't let the fear of hardships cripple us from moving forward into all God has for us. Yes, hardships of many kinds exist, but God's grace enables us to endure them. Pushing beyond fear activates a supernatural experience of God's manifested power and love in unprecedented ways.

Solid Food

> But solid food is for the *mature*, who because of *practice* have their *senses trained* to discern good and evil (Hebrews 5:14 NASB, emphasis added).

Reflect on the emphasized words: mature, practice, senses trained. Serving solid food to my child the first time was comical and messy. Before solids, he devoured milk through nursing or drinking a bottle. He knew by instinct how to attain nourishment through sucking and swallowing movements and techniques. Using a utensil with rice cereal while propped in a high chair to eat solids for the first time was foreign. I pried his mouth open because, seeing an approaching spoon, failed to signal it was time to eat. A bottle prompted his mouth to open – but this spoon? No. Eating solids was an acquired skill.

Once I finally forced open his mouth and shoved the solid food in, his usual sucking motions prevented consumption. His normal nursing pattern meant food gushed out and dropped down his chin and all over him.

We obviously refused to relent, and with practice, he trained his tongue and swallowing motions to eat and enjoy solid food. Additional processes followed his mastery of motions needed to eat solids. For example, we introduced one food at a time. Some we couldn't introduce until certain ages because of allergies and the maturity of his digestive system. The journey to digest solid foods signified my little boy was maturing.

The above scripture's analogy to solid food paints a picture of the process we walk with the Lord. Sins controlled me before Jesus confronted me. Then God revealed my sins weren't His will for my life and the great revelation sparked responsibility. God purged my rebellious ways and trained me to pursue His will.

Refining involved sacrificial decisions but, on the other side of obedience, I experienced a new kind of freedom. My hunger was quenched when I transitioned from milk to solids. God extended the patience of a gentleman through the process. The old patterns no longer gripped and enticed me because I recognized them and perceived their toxicity. My senses now reject old patterns birthed from evil because of years of training in consuming nutritious solids. I've learned to war at a different level of intensity and maturity.

Over twenty years in, God is still training my senses to discern good and evil, as Hebrews 5:14 depicts. The evil I encounter with my current maturity level is more deceptive and disguised than in previous seasons, yet, because of the years of waiting and practicing, God trained my senses to discern His voice, not that of strangers.

The waiting season gave me a heightened awareness. The more I've seen a specific evil spirit repeatedly, the more I recognize it. Now those spirits are easier to identify when they surface.

Think of it like this – when we briefly meet someone and see them the next day walking down the street, we probably won't recognize them, and walk right by. But the more we see the same face, we begin to recognize people. We'll know how they speak, how they walk, and what makes them frustrated.

It's especially difficult when we encounter something sinister and evil and are the only ones who see and discern it. During the waiting season, we'll inevitably see evil prosper. Instead of allowing others' darkness to frustrate us, consider this a time where God is training our senses to discern certain evil spirits and teaching us how to respond so they won't entangle us in the territory ahead.

Practice discerning and let the Lord (and not emotions) train you in what's good and evil. How? The deepest level of discernment is only revealed by spending quality time in God's presence. There He'll share His wisdom.

CHAPTER TEN
Avoiding Pit Stops

Predictable Danger

As I absorbed more and more "solid food" during the waiting period, God continued to chip away thoughts, behaviors, attitudes, and patterns that ran contrary to His original design for me. Warring to maturity means purging extra baggage while we wait. Trust me, where God is propelling us, will have no room for extra baggage.

On a different road trip from Memphis to Chicago, we ran out of windshield washer fluid. It's not wise to drive with no washer fluid in Chicago's unforgiving cold weather. Visibility was impaired from the bugs and dirt caked on the windshield after driving for hundreds of miles. Rain started falling profusely and I thought, "Great! Some relief with the rain washing it all off until we get some washer fluid."

Much to my surprise, the rain made our situation worse. It smeared a blanket of what I'll call "bug dirt" over our entire windshield. Then something unbelievable occurred. The driver's side wiper snapped and broke. A torrential rainstorm pounded from heaven and a predictable danger lurked behind our hazy view. We needed washer fluid, had a broken wiper, and couldn't see two feet in front of us.

In the same way, we enter places without the proper equipment and put ourselves in situations where danger is predictable. We aren't reading our word. We aren't praying. All our armor is laying in a pile on our floor and we subsequently crash and fall into sin. Then we do something incredible. We blame the devil. The devil had nothing to do with it. Our negligence in eating solid food and warring to spiritual maturity caused the fall.

The waiting period is a time to learn the tough lessons, avoid predictably dangerous situations, and refrain from making the same pit stops that hold us back from where God really wants to take us.

Pit Stops and Cleaning up Vomit

Thankfully we stopped and purchased new wipers and washer fluid at a familiar exit. We frequent this pit stop regularly on our trips from Memphis to Chicago where we visit family. It provided our usual food, snacks, gas, and most importantly, it had clean bathrooms.

How often do we also make unsavory pit stops at the same places along our life's journey in spite of the filth? We exit for familiarity, comfort, convenience, or safety, yet the pit stop detours God's destiny and, ultimately, becomes a distraction:

- That unhealthy relationship
- That toxic behavior where we keep yelling at our kids
- Shunning our spouses, refusing to admit when we're wrong
- That tendency to cut people off when they hurt or disappoint us instead of loving them as Christ

commands
- Pornography
- And a plethora of other pits stops

> As a dog returns to its vomit, so a fool repeats his foolishness (Proverbs 26:11 NLT).

Eating our own vomit isn't natural for humans. Yet, when we continually stop at the same unclean places we know are "foolishness," the bible compares us to a dog returning to its vomit. If we know a pit stop is foolish, clean up the vomit and cut it off. Don't leave it out so we can return.

Cut it at the root...whatever "it" is. My pastor cut off a dangerous pit stop when he deleted from the phone the number of the man with whom I had fallen into sin.

All parents have or will experience streams of vomit at hours of the night reserved for sleeping. When our toddlers suffer from a stomach virus and throw up in their bed at 2:00 am, do we tell them "It's okay" and lay them back in their own vomit? No, that's preposterous and repulsive. In fact, the smell and act of seeing someone vomit makes most gag.

When it's our children in the middle of the night we get up, bathe them, force hydration with liquid or Pedialyte, strip the bed, and wash the sheets. Maybe we even repeat the process in an hour if they throw up again. It's what parents do to care for their sick child.

Yet as adults we lay back down in our vomit or keep it to the side unwashed. Only the Father's power can cleanse permanently and leave no remnants of our sickness when we lay down. Unfortunately, too many Christians refuse to undertake the tough things and war past their pit stops in complete surrender. Flesh controls our willpower to bypass the familiar stops and we are satisfied returning to and laying on our vomit. The power of Jesus inside each believer often goes untapped and dormant.

Sound judgmental? Mirrors reflect my struggles, like my weight. The strength to pass pit stops can be obtained by breaking the desired behavior into manageable steps and building new habits day by day.

Messes weren't created overnight. I've learned to give myself grace. I resolve each day to do something tangible that moves closer to where God wants me to be. Losing 100 pounds overnight won't be realized, but I can decide to eliminate soda today and walk for 20 minutes. Small disciplined changes accumulated over time result in complete shifts.

The waiting period, when spent wisely, teaches us to visit cleaner pit stops equipped with all we need for the journey ahead. God permanently prunes and cleanses faulty attributes to better reflect His glory and inspire others similarly situated.

After years of laboring to avoid negative pit stops, we understandably sink into frustration, desperation, and defeat. No matter how hard we try, we continue returning. For some, the unbroken pattern exists because we fail to exert effort and sacrifice, resulting in a continual return to vomit. Been there, done that.

On the other hand, others are frustrated and defeated after travailing and pleading with God to take away that "pit stop." Every time you experience freedom, temptation is lurking to trigger a potential fall again. It feels like, "two steps forward, three steps back."

You may find yourself today desperate for freedom from the gripping sin entangling you; but nothing seems to work. Maybe you've spent countless hours researching ways to correct it and spent hundreds, if not thousands of dollars trying to rectify it.

Whether it's obesity/gluttony (the one that grips me), addiction, or mental illness (depression, anxiety, pornography, etc.), let's refuse to give up, no matter what stronghold holds us down. You are stronger than you realize because Christ lives in you.

Yesterday you may have quit. Today is a new day to battle. Don't dwell on what feels like the umpteenth time you've tried and yet failed.

I love an inspiring plaque displayed on my pastor's desk that reads, "Perhaps today." "Perhaps today" is the day God delivers you permanently with no return. Repent again today and focus on the one step you can take right now.

Resolve with righteous indignation to rid yourself of condemnation, guilt, depression, anxiety, and feeling overwhelmed, in Jesus' name. You can't get yesterday back, so leave it behind. But "Perhaps today" is your day for a miracle.

Bind whatever sin is holding you down and call the specific demonic spirit out by name. Repeatedly. "Depression, I command you to leave and bind you right now, in the name of Jesus." Call it (whatever "it" is) by name and believe God is able to heal and deliver you from oppression.

Here are a few spirits we have the power and authority to cast out: deception, lust, rejection, jealousy, idolatry, addiction, pride, fear, anxiety, doubt, mockery, witchcraft, and the occult.

The enemy loves to remind us of the countless times we failed. He uses vulnerabilities to place seeds of doubt and condemnation. I'm sure we've heard this saying: "when satan reminds you of your past, remind him of his future!" Trust and believe that God is fully able to perform His word and, when deliverance comes, walk in it. Guard and protect it!

CHAPTER ELEVEN
Walking Confidently and Humbly

Walking in High Heels

We have the Holy Spirit generator of power, we're warring with our words, we're sharpening our discernment senses, and not returning to unhealthy pit stops. Now it's time to walk in stride toward the promises God gave to us.

A good friend of mine underwent knee surgery, which caused an extended time off work with months of physical rehabilitation. The day after her surgery I went to her house and helped because she was barely mobile on her crutches.

With time, she slowly weaned off the crutches and one day (months later), I saw her walking at church with no limp and I was elated. When I expressed my excitement, she smirked and said, "Don't be fooled!"

While she looked "normal" outwardly, the limberness in her knee diffused all confidence to walk. She casually said, "I can't wait to wear high heels again." Her comment stuck to my spirit.

You see, while healing had taken place and she appeared to be back to normal, her ligaments still weren't strong enough. They could not support her full weight while walking in high heels.

She longed for her elegant classy look of yesterday. But the truth is she needed additional time to heal before she could elevate her stance again. "He heals the brokenhearted and binds up their wounds" (Psalm 147:3 NIV).

Isn't this reflective of life itself? We fall and get injured figuratively. Maybe during the waiting season we fell again and made some unwise decisions that weren't pleasing to God. Maybe something untruthful was exposed and we're dealing with the repercussions. Whatever the fall, we've all been there. "For all have sinned and fall short of the glory of God" (Romans 3:23 NIV).

Some slips and falls heal more easily and some take longer. God's power manifests some healing instantly and other times He allows a process. Some healing and recovery are accompanied by the pain and hurts God wants us to face.

Forgiving my mother took place immediately at a women's retreat. But my road to forgiving myself for sexual sins was a process.

My friend gradually learned to bear weight on her knee after travailing through agonizing encounters in rehab where it hurt to engage in rudimentary tasks like coughing or rolling over. So why do we expect emotional and spiritual healing to be quick and easy?

Yes, God can bind our wounds instantaneously but maybe healing is delayed as a result of our reluctance to go through the full extent of the pain necessary to recover.

Some self-medicate. Some bury the offenses deep inside and keep busy to stay distracted. We become numb and often bitter. We wallow in whatever injury or sin (past or present) is holding us back. These are dangerous traps that usually lead to a victim mentality.

Our injured and broken areas won't heal properly if we fail to take the necessary time during the preparation period to engage in the uncomfortable work of letting go. We'll parade through life damaged. On the outside, we may "fool" people that we're healed because we aren't "walking with a limp."

But in reality, on the inside our mending is superficial. We remain wounded and scarred. We're still wearing flats spiritually when God desires to see us model high heels. Spiritual high heels are awarded once we surrender to the painful healing process.

There's great news though...while recovery requires endurance and long-suffering through tender wounds, the cure is eternal. We must completely surrender to secure permanent wholeness and fullness in Christ.

It's hard. It may be a long painful process. It'll probably mean forgiving ourselves, forgiving others, and surrendering our hurts to the Lord. Allow the balm of Gilead to bind our wounds so you can kick off your flats and begin to rock high heel stilettos again (see Jeremiah 8:22).

How? Pray for the person who caused you hurt. May sound simplistic, but earnestly intercede for their needs and wellbeing. Maturity follows such obedience and self-sacrifice. As we pray for the person we need to forgive, our hearts will supernaturally soften and begin to release compassion.

In the wise words of our ultimate example, Jesus, when facing crucifixion by His enemies said, "Father, forgive them, for they do not know what they are doing" (Luke 23:24 NIV). Forgive while you wait.

Confident Humility
After you receive God's grace and deliverance and start

walking confidently on those high heels, don't be surprised if you become misunderstood and attract "haters." Your confidence in who you are in Christ will often be interpreted as arrogance. However, deep down inside the complete opposite may be true.

My confidence is rooted in a grace-filled humility because, despite who I am – the filth, the deceit, the insecurities, the ugliness – He still wants to and does use me. This reality fuels and gives me strength, confidence, and authority, even when I don't reflect His majesty. Even when I'm blemished.

Only God's coal on my lips can purify the words I speak and the motives behind my actions.

> He touched my lips with [a burning coal] and said, 'See, this coal has touched your lips. Now your guilt is removed, and your sins are forgiven' (Isaiah 6:7 NLT).

As part of my calling, I minister to individuals who've been trafficked and carry a lot of pain and trauma. Through my years in law enforcement at juvenile court and in non-profit management, people have confided things that caused them great shame and embarrassment.

Before ministering, I pray Isaiah 6:7 over my life...that God would touch my mouth with coal and purge anything inside me that would hinder His words from coming forth.

One night, while praying for someone I asked God for wisdom and was led to Hebrews 4:16:

> Let us then [meaning after we mess up] approach God's throne of grace with *confidence*, so that we may *receive* mercy and *find* grace to *help* us in our time of need (NIV, emphasis added).

When we mess up, it's difficult to approach God's throne with this confidence because we often feel guilt, embarrassment, shame, fear of consequences, or condemnation.

While confidence is imperative, it doesn't mean arrogance. There's a fine line. If we approach God's throne of grace with arrogance, I imagine it sounds something like this: "Well, I messed up again but it's okay because God will forgive me. He knows I'm weak in this area." God's grace doesn't grant us a free ticket to continue in our sin. Don't believe me? Reflect on Romans 1:1-7.

When we approach God's throne of grace with this arrogant disposition, we're taking advantage of and cheapening the grace given to us that Jesus paid for with His life. There was a cost for the grace entrusted to us. We didn't have to pay for it – but someone had to. Jesus did!

Approaching God's throne of grace demands true humility and gratitude. Not self-pity, condemnation, fear, or arrogance. When we approach His throne with this disposition (confident humility), that's when true repentance and change take place.

It may sound like an oxymoron, but we can be confident and humble at the same time. My confidence doesn't come from myself because then it would shift to arrogance. I am confident in who I am in Him because of His grace.

During the waiting period, God desires to develop an increased maturity in how we approach His throne of grace...with confident humility.

Refocusing your I

> So, whether you eat or drink, or whatever you do, do *all* to the *glory of God* (1 Corinthians 10:31 NIV, emphasis added).

At the end of my era of waiting, I experienced a catastrophic hurt I didn't understand. My prayers sounded something like this:

"God I was obedient when you told me to leave my six-figure job as an attorney and top administrator after 18 years at juvenile court to go into full-time ministry. Next, I was obedient when you told me to leave my relatives, church, and friends and move far away from Chicago where we knew no one.

Now I am here, in a foreign land and things didn't turn out the way I thought they would. What do you want me to do? I know I heard you correctly. Right? I thought it was crystal clear and we've been obedient."

With my face on the ground in intimate prayer, I pleaded for understanding and direction in what to do. My prayers were a slippery slope. I could've easily ended up in a victim, "woe is me," mentality.

It was then that I felt a nudging: "Stop focusing on what you did in obedience and start focusing on what I, the Lord God, did to open doors for you."

Yes, I was obedient and walked through the open doors. But my obedience was possible because God opened the door first and told me to move. The Lord gave me the opportunity to respond in obedience. After catching the ton of bricks that I was behaving self-centered, I reviewed my "I" with intentionality.

Instead of focusing on what "I" did to act obediently, I've chosen to refocus my attention and thank God for the opportunity to even be obedient. God doesn't need my obedience. The opportunity to respond in obedience is for me, not for Him. If I make the choice to be disobedient, He can find someone else for the assignment, who will be obedient.

When in an unexpected place, it's normal for our flesh to ask God, "Why?" Now let me pause and be frank: some of us are waiting or in a difficult season because of disobedience and our own doing. That's a whole different topic for another day. But maybe we're in a confusing place after God opened doors and led us there. And now that we're there, things just don't make sense.

You can choose to blame or question God…or question whether you heard God correctly. Or you can choose to praise the Lord for opening the door, trust in His sovereignty, and not lean on your own understanding (see Proverbs 3:5-6).

Resolve today to have this disposition despite your lack of understanding and disappointment. Trust that you're exactly where God wants you to be, even with all the unknowns and hurts. What you're experiencing is part of the journey. The big picture will unfold in time. Just remain obedient.

God doesn't change His mind. Man may, but God doesn't. He is the door opener and closer! Be obedient and then trust, listen, and learn. Rethink your "I" today and watch your mind shift.

CHAPTER TWELVE
Warring through Loneliness

The waiting season, if spent well, will purge unhealed places in our lives and also provide lessons that can only be learned in solitary, lonely places. During many years of waiting, I felt so unwanted, so unloved, and so alone.

Gary Chapman's book *The Five Love Languages*[6] will provide clarity in how we receive love. In my experience, every Christian's "love language" is shut off from people at some point during the waiting stage.

So, if I feel love when others give me affirmation, I'll probably go through a season where no one – absolutely no one – affirms me. If I feel loved through physical touch (like my husband and youngest son), I'll go through a season where no one will touch me and show me affection physically.

I believe we go through this absence of human love so we learn to rely on God alone to keep our "love tank" full, despite how others treat us.

But He answered and said, 'It is written, 'Man

shall not live on bread alone, but on every word
that proceeds out of the mouth of God' (Matthew
4:4 NASB).

In 2013, when I stepped out in faith and resigned from my
comfort zone at juvenile court to work in full-time ministry, I
went through a very solitary period. I obtained little to no
affirmation from my co-workers and the smallest things felt
like uphill battles. I was starting all over after working in the
same environment, with the same people for years. This
made me quickly realize my self-worth was very connected
and tied to others' affirmation.

This revelation perplexed me because, historically, I had
never encountered a lot of people affirming me. By the
nature of my position at juvenile court, I often experienced
more slander and jealousy than accolades. Even so, at least
one or two were in my corner validating me. Their minimal
affirmations pushed me forward and silenced the masses.

Then God strategically stripped away all affirmation for a
season. In no way is this a condemnation of those I co-
labored with in ministry. They are amazing. God exposed
my dependence to grow confidence and knowledge of who I
am in Christ, not in man. During these very low times, when
my husband and coworkers weren't affirming me, I learned
how to press into God and rely on His approval alone to
sustain me. The source of my joy, peace, value, and worth
had been tied to others' treatment and words and, without
positive reinforcement, I felt devoid of those qualities.

God intentionally turned off my "love language" from
man, so I could experience Him at a deeper level. It wasn't
easy; I felt desolate. I felt a void. I didn't want to love the
people who were withholding the affirmation, which is one
of my love languages.

But man cannot fill these voids: only God can. In fact, we put unfair expectations on man to fill voids when the power to sustain joy lies in Jesus. When we remain in God's presence during our loneliest seasons, He'll physically touch our hearts, minds, and soul and allow us to love, despite not feeling loved. The lover of our soul – God – will divinely touch us and make us complete.

During the waiting season (when my "love language" was turned off), I learned God's affirmation is sufficient. Man may slander and throw stones at me, but I do not live by the strength given through man but by "every word that proceeds out of the mouth of God" (Matthew 4:4 NASB).

We'll also inevitably find, the higher up we go in an organization, the lonelier it gets. When promoted to supervisor at juvenile court, my circle of friends instantly narrowed. As a person in authority, I had to hold previous peers accountable. In addition, as a supervisor, my access to confidential management information expanded. Suddenly I couldn't share things with people who were my peers the day before. I no longer vented frustrations with line staff.

When promoted to Deputy Chief – wow – my seclusion exploded! Not only did my circle get smaller, but many people were also extremely jealous and angry about the youngest and least tenured employee getting a position they had waited decades to receive.

Now I had access to even more confidential information and could no longer share things with peers at the supervisory level. My pool got narrower and narrower the higher up I went. This reclusive pool was initially difficult because, by nature, I was a people person who cared what others thought and felt.

I learned this valuable lesson through my secular success in organizations that the higher we go, the lonelier it gets horizontally with our peers but, the more intimate it becomes vertically with our heavenly Father. Now, instead of relying so much on my peers and what they think of me, I press into God with more vigor and encounter Him at a higher level than ever before. With a smaller circle, I've become more concerned about what God thinks of me.

Could it be that during our extended time in waiting for our revealed dream to manifest, God is teaching us how to war, not with man by our side, but with Him? He strategically shuts off our love language with man and narrows down our horizontal access with peers to refine and hone our skills of depending on Him completely. The strange thing is, something so intimate happens when we distance ourselves from humanity because it draws us closer to our Abba Father.

I'm not advocating for intentional long periods of isolation, which is a dangerous place. However, if you find yourself in a lonely space, find solace in the shadow of the wings of the Lord (see Psalm 17:18).

CHAPTER THIRTEEN
Breaking through Offenses

Our service in ministry can make us more susceptible to a sea of offenses including hurt, disappointment, and rejection. When Christians commit these offenses against us it's especially challenging because we have a higher expectation of co-laborers we consider brothers and sisters.

Many never recover from wounds inflicted by the church. There's no hurt like family and church hurt. Don't be caught off guard by it. The church is filled with imperfect people serving a perfect God.

During our seasons of waiting, we can learn to war past the struggle of holding on to offenses. Where God is taking us there's no room for past offenses that only weigh us down.

Offense of Rejection
During the waiting period, I faced a lot of rejection, to which I am vulnerable. What people thought of me used to control my thoughts and actions. The approval of others was a weight and plagued me when I perceived disappointment.

I'd lay and replay situations in my head that ultimately fed insecurities and led to assumptions.

However, through all the waiting seasons I learned to care more about what God thinks of me than others. The result? While I don't completely shut out everyone (because then I wouldn't be teachable) I filter (through discernment) the words of many, and discard those who are assassins.

How do you discern? Practice – which takes time. The more you encounter assassins, the easier they are to recognize. Jesus is now my litmus test.

No matter how difficult it is, we can train ourselves to not take things personally when people reject us. It happened to Jesus. Why wouldn't it happen to us? Maybe God is allowing someone to reject you because their acceptance would cause a delay in where God really wants to take you.

Stop trying so hard to get man's approval, when God's approval rating and measuring stick is the standard that matters.

> but just as we have been approved by God to be entrusted with the gospel, so we speak, *not to please man*, but to please God who tests our hearts (1 Thessalonians 2:4 ESV, emphasis added).

During years of reflection, I learned to develop thick skin, let things slide off me, and listen for God's feedback.

Often, seeds of rejection bear fruits of competition and jealousy because we see others receiving the acceptance we so desire. My family is the worst with competition. We are intense trash talkers, and always competitive when playing games or sports. We must exercise caution because there is absolutely no room for competition in ministry.

Competition says "one on one" with a goal to defeat and

win. A "one on one" competitive mentality in ministry doesn't lead to harmony. Competition in church breeds division and pitches us against each other, resulting in a lack of harmony. Whenever competition and jealousy rear their ugly head in ministry, we must root it out.

In addition to rejection, we will invariably encounter other hurts and disappointments that try to exploit our vulnerabilities. During pruning seasons, I became very familiar with my insecurities and can now recognize the signs when they surface. I've gained techniques to war against them so they don't control me. It's imperative that we know our weaknesses so others cannot take advantage of them.

Offense of Slander

Years ago a deep hurt was inflicted on me by someone in leadership at church who attacked my character. As a result, I honestly hated and didn't like being around this person. I blamed her for the situation I found myself. Every time I saw her posts on my news-feed, my thoughts were...well, let's just say, not too pleasing.

As a leader and student of God's word, I knew my sentiments weren't right. I told myself things like: "I love her because she's my sister in Christ...I just don't like her." What a subtle, deceptive lie!

After a month, God convicted me of the mandate to love her. My response: "God I don't want to love her. I don't even like her." I recognized I had to forgive her. After all, I taught forgiveness at retreats and in women's bible classes, so this should be easy. Besides, I'd been hurt so much deeper in the past, and overcame. Yet, I found myself over twenty years into the journey not knowing where to start. My anger consumed me for that month.

Then one day, while reading the word, I hear: "Start praying for her." Really? My initial prayers for her weren't too "holy" and, to be honest, were shallow. At the same time, as I genuinely made the effort to pray for her and her family, God did something miraculous. He started replacing the anger and hatred with compassion and – wait for it – love.

Notice the word "genuinely." If you're praying as a mere exercise but your heart harbors bitter feelings, start with asking God to help you pray from a genuine space.

Only in God's presence, can He remove stones in our hearts and give us hearts of flesh for someone who has hurt, violated, or offended us (see Ezekiel 36:26). Years have passed and we no longer serve in ministry together, but I can confidently say I love her. We regularly text and periodically call each other to share words of encouragement.

In retrospect, I'm actually grateful for the character assassination because it propelled me out of the nest to where God was beckoning. Without that sharp nudge, my loyalty to man would probably still have me planted there.

I've experienced the damage caused emotionally, mentally, and physically when we hold on to offenses caused by the things people say. It's normal to get hurt and angry and not like people. But God calls us to let go and not completely cut off the people who offend us. Instead, we pray for, forgive, and love even the unlovable.

It's easy to encourage and love people who are lovable. But can we love and encourage the one who offended us? Can we give up the right to be right and choose to see the best in people?

God asks us to put on the biblical mindset that persecution and slander mean "I'm blessed."

> Blessed are those who have been persecuted for
> the sake of righteousness, for theirs is the
> kingdom of heaven. Blessed are you when people
> insult you and persecute you, and falsely say all
> kinds of evil against you because of Me. Rejoice
> and be glad, for your reward in heaven is great;
> for in the same way they persecuted the prophets
> who were before you (Matthew 5:10-11 NASB).

Offense of Oppression

The gift and call on our lives will attract disguised assassins who use their power to oppress the gifts within us, sometimes without even their knowledge. The root of oppression is normally jealousy.

During one assignment, my supervisor actually told me he was jealous of me. Almost 100% of that temporary assignment consisted of writing.

It was a season where constant critiquing, criticisms, and sometimes insulting words were spoken. During that season nothing I wrote was good enough.

Don't get me wrong. It's not that I cannot take feedback or am not teachable. Or that I never have people read my letters, grants, or emails to make sure the content is clear and presented with excellence. We can always get better at our trade.

I've had some amazing teachers and editors throughout my career. I invited and had many people tear this book apart with grammatical and content edits that dramatically improved its quality.

No, it wasn't the feedback that tore me down. It was the oppressive and jealous spirit behind the words, coupled with many allied spirits trying to obscure where God was taking me.

By the time I had finished that assignment, my gift and love for writing was left damaged and scarred. All the negativity spoken into me left me discouraged and believing I was a terrible writer. A lesson I learned through it all was to ignore those whispered lies that fed my insecurities and instead listen to the God assignment given in the womb.

I learned to humble myself, think the best of people, and not take their negativity to heart. Instead, I took the nuggets they taught me through all their constant commentaries and released everything else. I replaced any frustration, anger, and resentment with honor, love, and compassion, and here's the key – I moved on.

People may be good-hearted with the best of intentions, but just not called to lead your gifts. On your part, choose to think the best of people, even when it hurts. Forgive, let go, and move on.

And seeing the wicked prosper should not surprise us. The prophet Jeremiah complained to God when he witnessed this apparent injustice:

> I would speak with you about your justice: why does the way of the wicked prosper? Why do all the faithless live at ease? You have planted them, and they have taken root; they grow and bear fruit. You are always on their lips but far from their hearts. Yet you know me, Lord; you see me and test my thoughts about you (Jeremiah 12:1-3a NIV).

Jeremiah complains and questions God's justice system. Then he shouts (denoted with every !) requests that almost sound like commands: "Drag them off like sheep to be butchered! Set them apart for the day of slaughter!"

(Jeremiah 12:3b NIV).

We're left hearing those exclamation points, which demonstrate the volume of his voice righteously dictating how God should handle the wicked.

God's response to Jeremiah's complaint found in verses 5-17 as well as Jeremiah 13:1-14 is a great read. Remember, He sees all things. The wicked can deceive man, but they cannot deceive God.

CHAPTER FOURTEEN
Bouncing Back

Maybe offenses or hurts aren't what God needs to heal.
Maybe we need freedom from failures and losses.

When Losing Keeps you up all Night

My son got a new football game for his PS4 and twice in a
row this then 11-year-old boy triumphed over his father
with a complete whooping. The sounds and trash talking
emanating from those games were fierce. Remember?
Competition and trash talking during games are regularities
in our family.

The day after these two losses, my husband woke up,
came straight to our son, and said something to this effect:
"Come on boy. I want a rematch. I was up all night thinking
about our game and I am not going to lose again."

My husband relived the lost games over and over and
rehearsed in his mind all the buttons on the controller that
were second nature to my son. I chuckled and thought,
"when losing keeps you up all night." I've fallen prey to this
phenomenon during my high school and college years when

I missed a goal in a soccer game and re-played the failed attempt all night in my head.

Mentally, my husband prepped and pumped himself up, determined he would not experience defeat again at the hands of a minor! In our journey to reaching God's promises, we'll inevitably experience defeat. We will fail. We will fall. We won't always come out on top. We might get fifth place.

The test is, how do we function under failure? Do we persistently wallow with a defeated mindset or do we get back up and try again? The process of waiting is designed to teach us how to persevere through failures and setbacks.

Joshua was one of the twelve who spied out the Promised Land (see Numbers 13:16-17). Only Joshua and Caleb returned with the right perspective: that God would deliver the inhabitants into their hands. The other ten spies spread fear with their reports, describing themselves like grasshoppers.

While Joshua failed to convince the masses, he gained favor with Moses for forty years in the wilderness, and he and Caleb were the only ones from their generation to enter the promised land (see Numbers 14:22:24).

However, entering didn't occur immediately. Because the people refused to believe the right report and because they didn't wait well (grumbling and complaining), an extended waiting period followed. Joshua and Caleb waited forty years to re-enter the Promised Land and not because of their wrongdoing. Moses and the former generation had to die before a fresh generation was permitted to enter.

Be careful to refrain from company who don't wait well or you may reap the consequences.

Notwithstanding their obedience, lessons were learned during their waiting period under Moses' leadership, lessons that Joshua and Caleb carried into their season of conquering and leading in the land of Canaan.

Don't let defeat during the wait keep you down or stuck. It's a choice. You can choose to align your outlook with what God has promised and not what the masses believe. They may not enter the Promised Land because they don't have the right mental attitude. My husband refused to accept defeat and came back determined, eventually beating our son.

When we fail to heal from offenses and losses, they have the power to leave us limp and functionless.

Learning to Smile Again

In 2017 I had an encounter with shingles. I have never felt this amount of pain, even when bearing three children. It presented in my ear affecting my cranial nerves and left me with Bell's palsy.

Minutes before walking into church service, the room started spinning and the entire right side of my face went numb. I had absolutely no function or control over it.

I couldn't smile. I couldn't raise my eyebrows. I couldn't open my mouth or move my tongue on that side. When I ate and drank, everything streamed down my face unless I held my lips closed with my hand and tilted my head to the side where I had complete functionality.

When chewing, I bit the inside of my cheek on the paralyzed side and I couldn't even feel the gnashing taking place inside my numb mouth. I had to grab my cheek and hold it out when chewing to avoid damaging the inside of my mouth. Even my taste buds were negatively affected.

Brushing my teeth became a messy chore. Streams of water constantly cascaded down my face. My speech was slurred. My eye nerves didn't function, causing my affected eyelid to not blink properly. My hearing in the right ear was entirely gone. I couldn't sleep on one side because the inside of my nose would collapse on itself and I couldn't breathe.

Do you have a picture of my predicament? I dreaded being in public because of my physical appearance and all the challenges described. I looked in my mirror and concentrated really hard, trying to make my muscles work for simple tasks like curling my lip to smile. The result? Only a half smile appeared on the functioning side. I thought I would never smile again.

Have you been so hurt by others (friends, family, or the church) that you're walking around with only half your face functioning, while the other half is slumped down because of nerve damage? I want to encourage you today to learn how to smile again.

My complete healing from Bell's palsy was almost instantaneous. I found myself in church again and during worship, I felt the right side of my face begin twitching. It was like a circuit flickering trying to come back on...zap zap zap zap. The healing sensation caused me to worship even harder.

I didn't care who was looking at me. My words of worship sounded something like: "God, I know you can heal me. Heal me now. Right here. Right now during my worship to you. Heal me. You are able." Zap...zap...zap...BAM! The twitching stopped and I moved my lip muscles to smiling position and – the right side curled up! My eyebrows were both rising.

My smile returned!

My brother, my sister, today God can heal those past offenses and hurts and you can learn to smile again. Press into worship, pray, and intercede for those who have wronged you, and again, give up your right to be right.

How do we learn to smile again? Forgiveness through love.

Level up

If forgiveness is connected to our offender apologizing, we're giving them the power to our freedom. Forgiveness is for me and has nothing to do with the actions, inactions, or responses of my offender. Retribution and revenge disguise themselves as solutions for wounds and disappointments. When we engage in these disguises, they breed roots of bitterness and unforgiveness.

Growth mandates forgiveness and if we refuse to submit to the process not only stagnancy, but, even worse, regression takes place. When I went through the difficult period of church hurt, the less I trusted the process of forgiving the person who wronged me, the less I grew.

So many scriptures command us to love our enemies and those who have hurt, persecuted, slandered or oppressed us. During a season of forgiving others, God reminded me that love is a fruit of the Spirit. I meditated on the word "fruit" and how fruit grow. Just like apples, oranges, and strawberries grow, so does love, because it's a fruit.

As we experience more of God's love, our love grows deeper and deeper for Him. It's a beautiful love affair. Another level of love always exists and we go a level up.

When I married my husband I loved him. Fourteen years in, I love him at a higher and deeper level than when we first got married. And ten years from now I'll look back at now and say, "Man, I thought I loved him then, but my love has grown deeper and deeper with time." With the passage of time, trials have strengthened our commitment to each other.

While waiting for God's dream to manifest, we can level

up and love those who hurt us in a deeper way. I am not advocating remaining in abusive work and ministry relationships. In those instances, we can leave, move on, love at a distance, and refuse to harbor contempt, bitterness, or anger in our hearts.

I love some from a distance because their mistreatment has necessitated boundaries. My love for them takes the form of intercession and maybe an occasional encouraging text. Love can exist with boundaries.

The deeper I go in ministry, the deeper the wounds, equating to the higher level of difficulty in loving. As we mature and grow in our journey with the Lord, our fruit of the Spirit, love, should grow.

We shouldn't have the same level of love as when we first got saved. The more seasons that pass, the more fruit and more love we should exert because God pruned the branches that didn't bear the fruit of love. Once these branches are trimmed, new levels of love can continue to bud.

While we wait, learn to push through offenses by leveling up your love.

Never Again
While freedom in forgiving is powerful, abuse shouldn't be ignored or allowed. Loyalty is admirable, but not to the point of abuse. And your loyalty to man should never supersede your loyalty to God. When it does, ministry or man becomes an idol.

A wise friend once counseled me after experiencing a "church hurt" and gave this wise advice: "Sometimes God allows you to be hurt so you can learn to boldly and confidently say, 'Never Again!'"

During the waiting period, we can learn to recognize toxic

patterns and situations we often find ourselves in and say, "Never again will I put myself in that position." Some things are out of our control, while others are predictable and avoidable.

I've learned it's okay to sometimes gracefully bow out honorably and refuse to move further away from God's promises. The Lord will clearly reveal His plans in His timing. We have a choice to repeatedly put ourselves in situations (for a plethora of reasons) or break free from patterns that consistently move us further from our destiny in God.

Saying, "Never again" takes courage, but on the other side of obedience is indescribable freedom.

CHAPTER FIFTEEN
The Art of Ignoring

In addition to forgiving through love, another strategy in moving on is learning what I call "the art of ignoring." Those with children or brothers and sisters understand the constant arguments with siblings bickering over petty things.

You know those arguments. She's not sharing. He told me my breath stinks. Her turn is over; it's mine (fueling 20 minutes of back and forth). She looked at me...really? Yes – we've all been there.

Parents, we are professional mediators. During one of these frivolous episodes in the car, I remember instructing my then eight-year-old middle child to ignore the small irritations of her siblings sitting right next to her, and enjoy the ride. Within minutes of ignoring the argument, her brothers' bothersome behavior subsided because they saw it wasn't working.

During one-on-one time I taught her this skill of ignoring. By not feeding into the annoyance, when the person sees it doesn't work, they often stop. Displeasure is a beast that usually wants to be fed.

What a novel idea to carry this same concept (the art of ignoring) into our own lives when the enemy throws annoying distractions and offenses! When satan and his demons see it doesn't work, those distractions and offenses die off.

If we fail to make a conscious choice to ignore those pestering whispers, inevitably we remain stuck in whatever emotion that wants to take root (anger, bitterness, doubt, hurt…the list goes on and on). Next thing we know, 32 years lapse, and when the topic is brought up, we're still triggered into a downward spiral.

Remember the lesson of dating ourselves and knowing our weaknesses? Wisdom tells us to remain alert to those things that trigger us, no matter how trivial. Let me illustrate.

I'd say I had two childhoods: one pre-divorce in Colorado and one post-divorce with a blended family in Chicago. These two childhoods were separated by three tumultuous years where divorce proceedings were taking place.

In retrospect, I know my parents only wanted what was best for me. Yet, as in all homes, mistakes were made along the way that caused deep-rooted misgivings. Whether we admit it or not, we all came out of childhood with some scars.

Thousands of dollars were spent on therapy during those years to try and lessen the damage. Nevertheless, I carried wounds into adulthood that only Jesus could heal.

Knowledge of my insecurities was imperative because God wanted to pluck them out at the root. My deepest emotions stemmed from inadequacy and rejection. To compensate I strove to be extremely independent and driven.

Dependence on others was a sign of weakness. Academics was pushed, with the natural progression of life being high school, college, and then graduate school. I always wanted to measure up and never felt good enough.

These were never the intended consequences because, again, my family wanted what was best for me. However, these were unfortunate byproducts of the ugliness in divorce.

During seasons of waiting, pause and ask God to reveal roots that need to be pulled out. Self-awareness is the first step. We cannot ignore offenses if they haven't been healed and remain unresolved. Only after restoration occurs are we capable of ignoring offenses.

Even after the roots of rejection and inadequacy were severed, the enemy still attempts to re-surface and open the wound. He likes to whisper things in my ears and use others to bring me back to a place of defeat.

I constantly fight battles of:

- What others think of me
- Trying to measure up
- Not feeling "good" enough
- Not wanting to depend on anyone for fear of rejection or disappointment

Practice and time have eased the sting. The key to walking in my healing is acknowledging the root and recognizing how the enemy tries to re-surface those past self-doubts. When false sentiments attempt to plant another root with a reminder of yesterday's pains, I've learned to be self-aware, introspective, and honest.

Take time to self-reflect and assess what triggers exist, so you can counter with ways to block anger, bitterness, hurt, shame, or whatever emotion they spark, from resurfacing.

The alternative is allowing them control over our lives to the point of retreating from projects that bring the insecurities to the surface. Or maybe lashing out at people after being triggered, when in reality it's really something internal, not the outside world.

It's normal for past wounds to surface. Release their control by binding them in the name of Jesus. When gripped, additional healing of unresolved issues may still need to occur.

God wants us to receive deliverance and healing in the name of Jesus so we're not crippled by those unresolved roots. We all have them. Know what they are, surrender them to Jesus, and walk in the fullness of Christ.

Be careful in our assessment. Just because something reminds us of painful emotions, doesn't necessarily mean we haven't been healed and forgiven those who hurt us. I remember one instance where I was reminded of a hurt and thinking, "Man! God, I thought I was over this and forgave that person."

Forgiving doesn't mean forgetting. What happened to me as a child cannot be erased, but I choose to forgive, love, and not project those experiences on every person who exposes a raw nerve. I must walk in my healing. I often ask God to help me walk in my forgiveness when things stir up those memories.

One of the devil's schemes is to resurrect suspicions in our healing or deliverance. A wise pastor once gave me these nuggets of wisdom: "Our past is where the enemy had victory. Therefore, we should only visit the past in two situations: one, for healing and two, to be used as a testimony for God's glory.

One technique that has helped my overly analytical mind

is to stop thoughts promptly when my mind visits the past for any reason other than the above two. Here's a novel truth – I can control where my mind starts and ends up. When I replay the past, I am in essence reliving experiences in which the enemy had victory.

But, it's over! I have victory in that area, in Jesus' name! From the inception of the disturbing thought, I intentionally replace it with the love and forgiveness I receive. When those past sentiments try to creep in, I "captivate every thought to the obedience of Christ" (see 2 Corinthians 10:5). If my thoughts don't align with what Christ thinks about me or the situation, I filter them out. Practice the art of ignoring. It will take intentionality in the beginning as well as practice.

Anything we feed grows. The older we get, the thinner our physical skin gets (causing many elderly to become cold easily). At the same time, the older we get, the thicker our spiritual skin should become. Ignore offenses so the devil will recognize he can't use those tactics anymore and let things slide right off. Worship those distractions away.

CHAPTER SIXTEEN
Who I Really Am

Another tactic of the enemy is for us to analyze and replay all the wrongs of those who offended us. During the waiting I've learned to meditate on all I am in Christ Jesus, shifting my attention off them and onto God's truths. And don't take the bait of distraction by focusing on the wicked prospering.

It's easy to say shift our focus and "move on," but how do we accomplish this practically? One way is by repeating what I call the "I AM's."

"I AM"
Every morning on the car ride to school our family declares "I AM" statements over our lives. We repeat truths out loud about ourselves: "I AM honest. I AM a good listener. I AM obedient. I AM healthy. I AM wealthy. I AM going to learn to ride my bike." And on days of tests for my school-aged children: "I AM going to get an A on my math test today."

When assassins try to offend us with something contrary to our "I AM," our disciplined truths help us to rebuke the lie, in the name of Jesus.

Fruit results from these daily affirmations that regularly help my children get through intimidating situations. My daughter repeated "I AM's" in her head during a difficult test when she was feeling discouraged. My son repeated "I AM's" on the mound while pitching his first baseball game.

One day during the journey of writing this book all my kids recited their "I AM's" and my then seven-year-old blurted out: "Mommy, you didn't do one." I instantly shouted above my self-doubt, "I AM AN AUTHOR!" The truth overpowered the overwhelming intimations and doubt about my assignment.

Remember how I shared my subconscious thoughts that resounded during the entire writing process: "You don't have anything new to say. It's all so basic. Your supervisors couldn't even trust your writing ability in a simple internal email," – along with many other whispers. The words you release into the atmosphere are spirit and they are life (see John 6:63).

Declaring the truth through spoken words that combat doubt has the power to penetrate through the lies. With repetition, our spirits begin singing a new tune, a melody of truth.

Speaking Life Verses

Another step is to reflect on our life verses we have committed to memory, and repeat them out loud to combat those weaknesses that try to whisper in our ears. For example, from the outset I shared how I am terrible at waiting, so one of my life verses is Psalm 46:10: "Be still and know that I am God" (NIV).

When I become restless in the waiting and want a detailed plan, I immediately combat the tendency with this life verse as soon as the thoughts enter my mind. Once I begin entertaining the thoughts, it becomes more difficult to dig myself out of the hole. My thought life spirals out of control. We can train and control our minds and determine where they will start, where they will go, and where they will end.

Write the life verse in the margin. It may be a verse for a season you're enduring or it may be a lifelong foundational verse.

Breaking through Generational Bondages

Another key area of warfare is learning to break bondages passed down from one generation to another in our family lineage. They could be divorce, addiction, a poverty mentality, a victim mentality, fornication, adultery, promiscuity, crime, or violence. Bondages plague all families but we have the power and authority through Jesus to break this cycle.

> Know therefore that the LORD your God is God; he is the faithful God, keeping his covenant of love to *a thousand generations* of those who love him and keep his commandments (Deuteronomy 7:9 NIV, emphasis added).

My husband and I were the first of his five siblings to get married in church. Three siblings prior to us eloped and came home married, either already pregnant or parenting. We were the first to get married by our pastor, at church, with my husband's parents as witnesses.

We prayed against this pattern being passed down from generation to generation, and declared through Jesus the curse would no longer impact our lineage. To the glory of God, after our prayers and marriage, my husband's baby brother and sister both did not elope and also got married at church with our families present. My father-in-law got to walk his youngest daughter down the aisle in a beautiful ceremony.

What's the big deal anyway? Without getting into the pervasiveness of the bondage, let me just say his grandfather had fifteen children with four different women with periods of multiple women and children in the same house. We refused to pass down this legacy to our children and our children's children, so we prayed and broke this bondage.

While waiting for God's purposes to manifest, pray and fast for those stubborn areas in your blood line passed down for generations.

CHAPTER SEVENTEEN
Hold on to the Promises

The most effective way I warred through the waiting period was by holding on to the promises. During the solitary seasons and what seemed like an eternity of waiting, we'll need something to hold on to, some type of hope to fuel when we want to give up.

> I have set my *rainbow* in the clouds, and it will be the *sign* of the covenant between me and the earth (Genesis 9:13 NIV, emphasis added).

One morning, I sat by a pond equipped with a fountain that reflected a rainbow on the water. Knowing rainbows in the bible are God's sign of His covenant, I immediately thought "promises."

A peculiarity, however, coupled this rainbow reflection. The actual fountain had no rainbow but the reflection clearly showed a rainbow. How could something be reflected that didn't actually exist?

I took a picture, sent it to two people and they saw the

same thing. So I wasn't crazy. I pondered how something was present in the reflection, yet didn't exist in the reality of what was reflected. Only a reflection of a promise – rainbow – was present. As I sat witnessing this abnormal visual occurrence, I thought "reflect on the promises."

What a timely revelation, given that my current reality was not reflecting the promises God had entrusted to me more than 20 years previously. I had been in a place of great discouragement. Despite my radical obedience to the Lord, I was going backward by worldly standards and further from the promises God showed me, not closer. Like this body of water, there was a promise but it was not reflected in my reality.

I started to journal, looked up, and suddenly the reality of the glorious rainbow moved into the actual fountain. Now the rainbow promise cascaded into both the reality and the reflection. The fountain sprayed radiant colorful rainbow water with a mirror image in the pool. Words and pictures didn't do justice to the grandeur of the sight and symbolism.

As I reflected on the promises of long ago, I was reminded that it's imperative to hold on to and reflect on the promises during seasons when circumstances don't make sense and things appear opposite of what we see.

Our current reality may not reflect the promises of God and look the polar opposite, but my brother and sister, hold on to the promises He revealed. Our clutch is critical to our warfare.

> He remembers His covenant forever, the promise
> He made, for a thousand generations
> (1 Chronicles 16:15 NIV).

We aren't forgotten. We aren't overlooked. God isn't

playing favorite even when we see others less obedient prospering.

Fervently pray for God's promises and for an attentive spirit to hear. We'll need glimpses of His promises when going through the valley of waiting as a reminder that the pit isn't our destiny. It's just a "pit" stop on the way to the palace. And rest assured, we'll need every lesson from the journey to fulfill His promises. God doesn't waste any experience.

In the time span of eternity, the manifestation of God's dream is closer than we think. He is a suddenly God. Be still and trust in God's perfect timing. The promises revealed yesterday will move into our current reality in His perfect time. We will be in awe when the majesty of what only He can do becomes our reality. In the meantime, we must ask God to keep our hearts reaching forward to His magnificent promises.

> For the vision is yet for the appointed time; It hastens toward the goal and it *will not* fail. Though it tarries, wait for it; For it *will* certainly come, it *will not* delay (Habakkuk 2:3 NASB, emphasis added).

Hold on to the certainty promised. When I received a small glimpse of the enormous dream at the leader's conference I was not ready for it to materialize. But the snippet motivated perseverance through the many mountains and dry valleys.

Soon after receiving the glimpse, my secular career quickly started advancing. Yet, I never forgot the dream God had shown me at that conference. His favor opened great doors of opportunity. Yet, this favor came with a cross – a cross of jealous people all around me. I was slandered and misunderstood all the way to "the top."

Our character will be slandered and we will be misunderstood by a spirit of jealousy attached to people surrounding us. Jealous peers (or those seeking to get to our level) are relentless in besmirching our name. And jealous spirits who supervise us do the same – lie and slander, and use their position of authority to oppress or take credit for anything we put our hand to.

God spoke to Joseph in a dream, which made his own brothers jealous. They mocked him, threw him in a pit, plotted to kill him, and eventually sold him as a slave.

> When they [his brothers] saw [Joseph] from a distance and before he came close to them, they plotted against him to put him to death. They said to one another, 'Here comes this dreamer!' (Genesis 37:18-19 NASB, parentheses added).

They mocked and plotted against his dreams.

The closer we get to God's promise, the more deceptive the lies and slander become. Jealous people disguise themselves with the appearance of truth and have a "form of godliness" (2 Timothy 3:5), meaning the slander and lies they spread will be perceived as good. The same scripture warns us to stay away from such people.

Early in my career, the slander against me was so blatantly obvious. It was easy to refrain from defending myself because, quite frankly, they did a great job of making fools of themselves. But the closer God brought me to His purposes, the more discernment it took to recognize those who were jealous and the more wisdom I needed to articulate my responses.

The best advice from personal experience is for us to keep our mouths shut and not feed the jealous spirit that has a form of godliness. When we take the bait of defending our character or trying in whatever way to fix the damage caused, we're actually feeding into the jealous spirit. Don't consume the bait.

You have a high call and a high vision. Rest on the pattern of favor over your life and, during those arid lonely valleys, revisit God's promises that define you. The lies, slander, and deception do not define you. God's promises do. The vision He gave you, may tarry but it has an appointed time – wait patiently for it (Habakkuk 2:3).

In the meantime – when jealousy knocks, respond with love, humility, honor, and earnestly (with a pure heart) pray for those who persecute you. This isn't easy but what if getting to your promised land – your dream – involved getting persecuted and slandered?

It happened to Jesus, by the religious people. In the same way, it will happen to you. Man can attack your dream all they want. But God is the Dream Maker. Trust in Him.

CHAPTER EIGHTEEN
Character Counts

Not only do we need to learn to war at new levels, the preparation and waiting stages of our journey is a time to earnestly ask God to build upon or remove character traits that will sustain integrity and obedience in our assignments. Character counts where God is taking us.

In the Appendix, many character goals and character flaws are listed that may help along your journey.

One exercise I found beneficial was having 5-8 individuals who I worked with in various capacities (family, friends, co-workers, ministry co-laborers) complete an anonymous survey with questions tied to my character.

Was I trustworthy? Dependable? Person of my word? Did I take care of my health? I learned a lot about my strengths and weaknesses through this process.

Cautionary advice if you partake in this self-reflection: don't use the feedback as a discouragement, but instead to empower forward movement into all God has for you. Feedback is healthy when taken in the right spirit.

Character Development: Attitude Alternator

Waiting for something we want (or feel we are somehow entitled to), ultimately draws out our true character. True colors came out when under pressure and in seasons of doubt or drought. When God puts His plans for us on hold, what character comes out of us?

All cars need an alternator. The alternator generates electric power for our cars and keeps our vehicles charged. As a car is running, the alternator charges the battery and provides the needed electrical power to other systems.

A few common symptoms of a faulty alternator are: the lights can go dim or flicker, the car can stall or have difficulty starting, or the battery can die.

During the waiting period and beyond, our attitudes serve as an alternator to keep our vision positively charged. When we have a poor or faulty attitude (just like a faulty alternator), we'll have no power to keep ourselves charged.

A poor attitude will cause our lights to dim and flicker and we will lack the motivation to continue warring for the revealed dream. With time, a persistently bad attitude causes many dreams to stall and fade away.

Some of the most common faulty attitudes during the waiting and preparation seasons are complaining, frustration, anger, mistrust, pride, and doubt. I've experienced all of these attitudes in varying degrees and lengths of time.

They were all traps to keep me stuck in the wilderness. Feel free to add any additional faulty attitudes to the margin as a sign of your release.

During one especially trying season, I remember my husband saying to me, (after we finished complaining to one another): "I refuse to be like the Israelites and wander in the desert for forty years because of a complaining and poor attitude."

My attitude was a choice. The natural tendencies of these faulty attitudes invaded daily, and often hourly. I had to choose to entertain them or shut them out. Every frustrating assignment and person was designed to prepare my character for God's greater purposes to come.

I learned to temper my attitude under the Holy Spirit and ask for God to grace me with the patience to learn the lessons in every frustration.

On the surface our current reality may not make sense. We must trust we are exactly where God wants us to be and this season will both expose flaws and nurture great character traits for God's future assignments. If we aren't careful we will pray away the blessing that is tied to our current assignment. Let's stop treating the process like a curse. We may not see it now, but, trust me, with hindsight most of it will probably make sense.

For example, one frustrating season that occurred during my tenure at juvenile court was when my director assigned me to lead the department's financial division. The supervisor was going on maternity leave and I had five days to learn the entire complex County procurement process to manage our $40 million dollar budget.

I felt completely lost, overwhelmed, incapable and frustrated. One day in the middle of this assignment I complained: "God! I did not go to law school to be an accountant!"

Years later the purpose of this assignment was revealed when I became the executive director of a Christian non-profit. I needed all the budgeting and accounting lessons I learned during that frustrating season to manage the nonprofit and not be intimidated when applying for grants and managing millions of dollars.

Don't despise seasons that don't make sense. Trust that God knows all the skills and attitude lessons you'll need. He will carry over all you learn to benefit His future kingdom purposes. He recycles and wastes nothing.

During the waiting season, I also encountered seasons of being oppressed and misunderstood. I watched others (with little to no character) prosper. While I pridefully thought I was a better judge, I learned to humble myself and stay focused on the bigger picture of what God promised. Anything less, would cause an expense of unnecessary emotions and ultimately lead to delays and wasted kingdom time. God knows what He is doing. Submit to the process.

My waiting period also gave me an attitude of perseverance, and quenched doubts. The longer I waited and the further I got from the revelation I had at that leader's conference, the harder it was to hold on to, much less remember all the details. Hence the importance of writing down the dream.

When God first revealed His purpose for me, it was so clear and there was such an exhilaration. Ten years later I felt beaten up, with little to no flame alive. There were many occasions where I questioned whether:

- I had heard God correctly
- He had changed His mind or
- He had forgotten about me

The years of waiting taught me to wrestle with doubting myself and doubting God's provision. If faith was easy, we wouldn't need faith.

Our instant gratification society doesn't help during our term of waiting when we can: microwave food within minutes, learn about world news or friend updates instantly through the Internet and social media, and rely on an app to give us the information we need about anything around the world at a touch of our finger.

God doesn't operate as a microwave, Google search, or app. He believes in a refining process that'll purge impurities with time. If He was a Google search, we would see the spinning symbol in an endless loop. I've developed an attitude of: "Anything easy is not worth having."

> Nothing in the world is worth having or worth doing unless it means effort, pain, difficulty...I have never in my life envied a human being who led an easy life. I have envied a great many people who led difficult lives and led them well. Theodore Roosevelt

We'll probably also experience a time where it seems like everyone else around us is moving forward, while we remain stuck. A young woman I mentor from another country was in the United States on a Visa, while she attended an academic Christian program.

She was in her third year of the program, which was an internship. Her classmates were all working locally and traveling to different states where they were compensated. She couldn't travel or receive compensation because of her Visa status.

Many times she was left in the dorms all alone while her classmates were traveling and earning experience and finances to pay for their tuition. At first she contemplated leaving and going back to her home country. She didn't see the purpose of staying if she couldn't get the full experience out of the program.

She fought through those urges because God doesn't

change His mind. He brought her to a third year for a purpose and, while it did not turn out the way she expected, that experience was exactly what she needed.

During this time, where she wasn't getting the same experience compared to others, God was teaching her to: never give up, persevere to the end without a complaining spirit, and enjoy the ride. Just because it wasn't the same experience as others, doesn't mean it wasn't her full experience.

This woman has a huge international calling to preach to the nations. When she speaks, there is a tremendous anointing. I've observed people with higher anointing usually encountering a bigger desert tied to a bigger promised land. She fits this mold.

Not that she is better than others, but God gives a different amount of talent to different people. What this woman will need for her promised land is more intense than what others may need. So her wilderness, waiting experience is preparing her for the destination specifically assigned to her.

Could it be God has us waiting, while others are moving forward because we still have lessons to learn? Lessons we will need in our destination while others may not? We need to stop comparing ourselves to others who have their own path and journey. We're going to places specifically assigned to us and will need all the lessons only waiting can produce. Trust and submit to the Dream Giver's process.

As part of the journey, expect curve balls and remain flexible. This posture will curtail the urge to complain when circumstances don't go according to how we envisioned.

In life, there will be seasons of being on "play" and seasons of being on "pause." Letting God be the finger to press the "play" or "pause" button is critical. Because, if He paused us and we circumvent the pause and hit play, we are starting the movie or music in our timing ahead of His.

It's how we respond when He has us on the "pause" waiting mode that will determine the course of action for the "play." For those who are visionaries and builders like me, being put on "pause" can be wrenching. But the response in the "pause" builds the character needed for the "play." I'm now committed to removing my fingers and letting Jesus play the music.

Moving beyond Inspiration

During the span of waiting and preparing, God will show us the difference between inspiration and implementation. Inspired people don't experience lasting change simply by receiving an impartation. Their pattern consists solely in getting inspired for the moment, but taking no real action to implement it long-term; then they move on to the next "feel good" impartation. Inspiration with no action may feel good but results in no change.

For example, I've been in services where I felt really inspired to make a necessary change, like eating healthier or reaching out to that unsaved family member more. I may leave service, call that family member a few times that week, but once the inspiration wears off, I go right back to where I was before the inspiration.

Implementers, on the other hand, take their time when inspired by an impartation. They've developed an attitude that implementing God's plans will take intentionality, time, stretching, as well as some kind of sacrifice and character change. They move beyond the "feel good" inspiration and translate the impartation into action.

I regularly ask God what He wants to impart in my life during a waiting season. Will it inspire me for the moment or change and propel me over the long-term?

God never reveals and imparts things to hurt us. He wants to grow us so we can be better equipped for His service. Fight the urge to just be an inspired Christian. There are a lot of inspired dreams in graveyards that died without moving from inspiration to implementation.

While no one is looking, God is assessing our dispositions and attitudes. Are we:

- Inspired and sitting on the sidelines with a lax attitude?
- Appearing to have a great attitude, but on the inside having a heart filled with rocks?

Take some time to self-reflect and ask God to remove and replace any faulty alternators we may be carrying inwardly or outwardly. Embrace waiting with joy and expectation for when God propels us into implementing His God-sized dreams in unchartered waters. And position yourself for that moment.

Motives Matter

God is not just concerned about refining my attitude during the waiting season and beyond. He's also exposing and tempering my motives to align with His will. In our social media dominate age, one area in which God is watching my motives is through the content of my posts.

What appears as an innocent post to the majority of viewers may have hidden agendas. I'm always skeptical of individuals who have to post about everything they're doing.

> Beware of practicing your righteousness before men to be noticed by them; otherwise you have

no reward with your Father who is in heaven. So when you give to the poor, do not sound the trumpet before you, as the hypocrites do in the synagogues and in the streets, so that they may be honored by me. Truly I say to you, they have their reward in full (Matthew 6:1-2 NASB).

Pause and be honest when posting. Ask, "Am I posting to draw attention so man will see the good works I'm doing?" While there may be a pure aspect of our post (because what we did was genuinely from our heart) there may also be self-motives. When we post with even partial self-motives (even when there is a genuine intermix), be honest, we're still shifting some of the glory to ourselves. In essence, we are using that platform to fill insecurities – what I call, the "need to be needed."

Here are a few questions we can use to assess whether there's even a hint of ulterior motive in what we're posting:

- Do I want someone specific to see this post or is the post directed for anybody to see?
- Am I posting for any ounce of self-recognition or to promote some good act I have done?

While we may have the best of intentions and purest of motives with a post, it's also important to think about how our posts will be perceived or impact others. Be sensitive to others, even if in our heart we mean no ill will or harm.

There was a season where I started to post something that had no ulterior motives whatsoever. But I stopped and refrained from posting merely because of how it could've been perceived due to events that had just transpired. My heart was pure, but I wanted to be careful not to plant any seeds that could be misconstrued.

Ultimately, we need to find the right balance, because we can't be so consumed by how our posts are likely to be interpreted. Just be sensitive and use wisdom. That post may be just the right words someone needed to hear.

Don't get me wrong; there are great benefits to social media. Moving so far away from any family and our closest friends, I find great pleasure in sharing, seeing, and keeping connected through group sharing. However, there is often a false illusion of intimacy and inherent danger behind posts.

Others may not know or see our motive, but God sees and knows all things. "You know when I sit down and when I rise up; you discern my thoughts from afar" (Psalm 139:2 ESV).

If there's even a hint of any self-promotion or risk of being misunderstood, my advice is to err on the side of caution and refrain from posting. It could mean an extended period with no posts because, if we're honest, there are motives attached to our posts. A great alternative (so we stay connected with the people we wanted to share the post with) is to send a group text or email. Or pick up the phone and truly connect.

Humble Gifts

I have not only seen individuals use social media to draw attention to their good deeds, but I've also seen Christians using their God-given gifts to fill a void of insecurity. For example, we may have a high anointing to pray and intercede for others, so much so that we are often asked to lead in prayer, where supernatural things are revealed and people break down and are healed.

If we're honest, it feels good to be used by God and have His gifts manifest through us. Be careful though to not use the gifts God gave you to fill any void or make you feel good about yourself.

God gives us gifts to glorify Him and draw people to Him, not to us. During the waiting period, learn the invaluable lesson of humbling your gifts to the authority and power of the Gift Giver.

I am constantly asking God to expose my insecurities so I am self-aware and can war against them, as discussed earlier. Any remnant of me in exercising my gifts is a form of idolatry because I am putting my insecurity above God.

The spiritual gifts God has entrusted to me are for His glory, not to fill my insecurities. "To God be the glory" is not some trite expression. It should be the DNA of every Christ follower. False humility and using spiritual gifts God has given to compensate for lacks can also become a form of pride. I am projecting confidence on myself about something I have absolutely no control or power over.

Our motives matter. God looks at our hearts. I want to say with confidence: "For your Glory, 100%" with no percentage returning to me.

Communicating Character

A large part of our character is displayed in the way we communicate. While waiting, God will give us a lot of practice in learning effective and Godly ways to communicate, including saying nothing at all. Yes, we can communicate character through silence. Just because something is playing out in our head, doesn't always mean it needs to be projected.

Those who can't wait have a sense of urgency which comes through in many ways including their body language, words, and actions. We've all seen the person visibly anxious while waiting. They pace back and forth, sigh deep breaths, constantly look at their clock. Their body language displays their inability to cope.

Someone lacking patience can completely change the atmosphere in a room just through their body language. It's almost contagious.

Then there are those who in frustration and impatience lash out with their words when they refuse to wait. It's almost like watching a grown-up throwing a tantrum. They're professional complainers, play the blame game, and maybe even make threats or try to manipulate others with words to get what they want quickly. Individuals using their words in impatience are also toxic and consuming to an environment. The whole world begins revolving around them and their demands.

Lastly, the actions of those who can't wait are impulsive and lack logical sense. Because the person wants what they want right now, they will act irrationally and make decisions that aren't well thought out.

All these behaviors may sound extreme for adults and sound more like adolescents, but some carry these tendencies beyond childhood. Unfortunately, I've seen 16-year-old children trapped in 45, 55, and even 75-year-old bodies.

By contrast, there's something so calming, peaceful, and endearing when in the presence of someone who knows how to wait well. Their character communicates faith and they are a joy to be around.

When we aren't getting our way, when God is silent, and we don't understand God's plan, our character can be refined as evidenced by the way we communicate. Through much practice and elapsed time, I strive to reflect the endearing qualities of someone who knows how to communicate patience in waiting.

Other areas in the waiting game that God wants to settle

in communicating character are being a person of our word and communicating effectively and clearly to those in our circles.

As I matured with time I learned from the mistake of not being consistent in word and deed. Early in my journey I often found myself changing my mind because I didn't wait for a well thought out plan and instead communicated too soon. Because I committed prematurely, I'd have to backtrack and sometimes go back on my word. This reflected poorly on my character and didn't build trust. Through hard lessons, I have become a woman of integrity in my words and commitments.

Gossip

In my humble opinion, one of the most toxic character flaws in communication is gossip. When someone spends time telling me intricacies about someone else, I cringe. I've even taken the bold step of asking my supervisor in love: "You sharing about everyone all the time makes me feel really uncomfortable. It also leaves me asking 'What are you saying about me to someone else when I am not around?'"

Slander returned back to me is gossip. And gossip is like yeast. A little can corrupt the whole body.

The bible has much to say about a person with a gossiping nature. Here are just a few: Ephesians 4:29, Proverbs 16:28, Proverbs 20:19, Proverbs 11:13, Proverbs 18:8, 1 Timothy 5:13, Exodus 23:1.

One area God exposed to me as it relates to gossip is, be careful when I "vent." This truth may pertain more to women, but I (like most women) process by talking things through with someone. When something happens, my natural instinct is I need to talk about it and, through that, receive insight.

However, in the development of my character, I've learned to be cautious when "processing." Processing things with others in actuality can be a form of gossiping. I can label it "venting" or "processing" but nine times out of ten, it's gossip.

My first response now when I need to "vent" is to process with the Lord in prayer to get things out of my system. If I still need to process and seek counsel, I try and ask someone who has no relationship with the parties involved. I want to avoid planting seeds in anyone close to the parties involved that could give them a judgment about that person in the future.

Communicating Encouragement

My continuous prayer is for my character to communicate genuine encouragement to others. Being a positive encourager will attract like-minded positive communicators who will serve as tremendous assets when living in God's dream.

> But encourage one another day after day, as long as it is still called 'Today,' *so that* none of you will be hardened by the deceitfulness of sin (Hebrews 3:13 NASB, emphasis added).

This scripture is so powerful! The statement "so that" is, in essence, the "why" behind the instruction to encourage others daily. "So that" discloses my encouragement is not just for the encouraged – but is equally, if not more, beneficial for me as the encourager. Encouraging others is the medicine for my heart (as the encourager) to prevent it from hardening. It makes sense.

Whenever God has used me to encourage someone, no matter how small, there's something so gratifying that takes place. Not that I took ownership of the encouragement with the motive of getting something in return. But that despite my flaws, God can still use me to bring encouragement to someone else. Any part that God can use me in releasing encouragement to another, wow! It's humbling and keeps my heart soft.

And be honest – it feels good to see others encouraged and not living defeated lives. And, if that doesn't feel good, then let me be frank: maybe there are pieces of our hearts that are hardened. And maybe, just maybe, encouraging someone daily is the antidote to hardened egos. Allow me to tread even a little deeper.

Take the challenge to not just encourage the person who is "easy" to encourage. Encourage that one person who gets under your skin, the person who you don't think "deserves" to be encouraged. That one. If Jesus thinks they're worth encouraging, shouldn't we, as followers of His?

While writing this book, I've had to pause to send a genuine note of encouragement to someone who hurt and disappointed me profoundly. And not just sending a text and checking that off my to-do list to be obedient to the word. No. I had to ask myself, "What was my heart behind the text? Did I mean it? Was it genuine?" Giving genuine encouragement keeps our hearts and minds in a positive frame.

For those of us on social media, this is a good litmus test: when we scroll through timelines and see a certain person's post, does it conjure up any emotions that are less than wholesome? If so, that is someone we need to love, pray for, and send encouragement to today. Don't delay.

Did you gloss right over that word of wisdom and not say a prayer or send an encouraging text to someone outside your circle? Pause. Try it. Your pleasant words could be just what the person needs this very moment.

> You have heard that it was said, 'You shall love your neighbor and hate your enemy,' But I say to you, love your enemies and pray for those who persecute you, so that you may be sons of your Father who is in heaven" (Matthew 5:43-44 NASB).

What is the opposite of encouragement? Discouragement. The enemy knows this truth about the double impacting power tied to our encouragement of others: the power not just to impact the life of the person we're encouraging, but also the power our own heart by keeping it from hardening.

It should, therefore, come as no surprise that one of the enemy's tactics is to bring discouragement to us as the encourager. Because when we're discouraged from encouraging someone, it leaves that person with a void, deprived of the gift we possessed. So now instead of double power (we and the encouraged being impacted), we have double defeat – a discouraged encourager and a discouraged recipient.

One day without encouraging someone can be enough for hearts to be deceived by sin and harden. The person I sent the encouragement who hurt me never responded, but that's not my responsibility. I am only responsible for my obedience when God calls me to genuinely encourage someone. Leave the rest at the cross.

CHAPTER NINETEEN
Personal Stewardship and Stewarding Others

Part of our character development during the waiting stage is learning to steward our gifts.

> But thanks be to God, who always leads us in triumph in Christ, and manifests through us the *sweet aroma* of the knowledge of Him in every place. For we are a *fragrance of Christ* to God among those who are being saved and among those who are perishing (2 Corinthians 2:14-15 NASB, emphasis added).

One day while strolling around my neighborhood I reflected on the word stewardship. I asked myself, "How am I stewarding my anointing?" I thought about the things I steward well and those I don' t – one of which is my physical health. Hence, I walked back and forth on our cul-de-sac and chose a marker on each side to ensure I made it all the way through and didn't take any shortcuts.

On the second pass, I noticed two markers in the street

were lids that were both labeled "sewer." Seeing the word "sewer" at the same time as meditating on all the things I wasn't stewarding well made a great impression. It was as if God was telling me: "Those things you're not overseeing well smell terrible to me – like a sewer."

In the middle of trying to gain ground in the area where I was failing – my health – I began picking up the pace and went longer than the goal I'd initially set.

I don't want to be a stench to the Lord. I want to emit a "sweet aroma" through God leading me in "triumph in Christ," as our scripture today promises.

Merriam Webster's dictionary defines stewardship as:

> "the conducting, supervising, or managing of something especially; the careful and responsible management of something entrusted to one's care."[7]

As an example, we're all commanded to steward our body well (which is a temple of the Holy Spirit) and our finances (so we can be a blessing to others). We also all have assignments we're uniquely entrusted to steward. These are the things we're anointed and appointed to accomplish. It's the things that come naturally to us.

Stewardship will undoubtedly require sacrifice, determination, and perseverance. All these character traits will blossom with the passing of time. And when we don't steward things well, we're in essence allowing a stench to rise to our Father's nostrils. When we manage the gifts bestowed upon us well, we're a fragrant offering.

Today we can draw our poor stewardship out of the sewer and put our actions back in God's hands. We must take consistent intentional steps to steward them well. And don't be surprised if God asks us to sacrifice your favorite thing to steward so it doesn't become an idol.

Lamenting for your World

Not only do we need to steward ourselves, we also need to steward our larger community well. Learning to lament for my city was one of the greatest character traits I learned while waiting for God's dream to materialize. When I stopped trying to figure things out for my own life, and instead focused on the lost and hurting around me, somehow my struggles in waiting diminished.

My oldest son has such a keen sensitivity to those around him, compatible with his name Noah, which means comforter. I call his gift "hospital eyes" because of an encounter he experienced early in life.

His grandfather, with whom he's very close, was going to have open heart surgery. The night before the surgery he was on a floor where children were allowed, so we took our three children to visit. Noah was around seven years old and had never been inside a hospital.

Patient's doors were open, and I observed Noah peering in, room after room, as we walked down the hospital corridor. He saw many patients laying almost lifeless with machines attached, which was all foreign to him.

Knowing how Noah internalized everything, I went to his room that night to ask how he was doing. He responded his usual "fine," but as his mom, I knew better. He eventually confided (with tears streaming down his face) and blurted out: "Mom! They're all going to die." He was greatly grieved by the plight of others.

There are people in our world we pass every day who are hurting and dying inside. Their decaying condition may be obvious like those we witnessed in the hospital. But I often pray for God to bestow me with "hospital eyes" so I can plainly see those around me whose sickness and death may not be visible to the naked eye. And I don't merely want to see them. I want to empathize and grieve with them...to lament with and for them and be a light.

The Merriam Webster's Dictionary defines lamenting as: "to mourn aloud: wail."[8]

When we see others in pain and suffering in bondage does it grieve us? Do we genuinely hurt for others?

I remember being at a women's conference where the speaker at the end of her powerful word did the typical thing that concludes most messages. She asked everyone to close their eyes and began praying. What happened next was anything but typical because when God intervenes, atypical things often take place.

She fell to her knees on that alter, with her arms open wide. Buckets of tears began streaming down her face as she prayed and interceded for people in that huge auditorium. I sensed at that moment she was feeling the gravity of sin in the room that was weighing God's beloved children down.

She was lamenting and crying out to the healer, Jesus Christ, to supernaturally come down and touch every iniquity and break every chain. Many people were healed that day through her bold lamenting and powerful intercession.

I also believe many didn't understand what they were witnessing that night and may have missed out. The priest Eli mistakenly thought Hannah was drunk when in reality she was lamenting because of her barrenness (see 1 Samuel 1:12-17). Only an infertile woman can understand that deep inner groan of pain. A lament I know all too well.

When was the last time the state of our cities grieved us to the point of lamenting? Do we casually watch the news and look at the state of our nation displayed through social media with no deep inner stirring to spiritual action? If there was ever a time where our world needs intercessors to lament and intercede, it's now.

> As [Jesus] approached Jerusalem and saw the
> city, he wept over it (Luke 19:41, NIV,
> parentheses added).

When the city of Jerusalem came into Jesus' view, He wept over it. He saw with spiritual eyes something that grieved Him. He didn't shed a few token tears. He wept. He lamented over the condition of the hearts of the people in the city. I love the Amplified Version of Hebrews 5:7-9 that reads:

> In the days of His earthly life, Jesus offered up
> both specific petitions and urgent supplications
> for that which He needed with fervent crying and
> tears to the One who was always able to save
> Him from death, and He was heard because of
> His reverent submission toward God His
> sinlessness and His unfailing determination to do
> the Father's will. Although He was a Son who
> had never been disobedient to the Father, He
> learned active, special obedience through what
> He suffered. And having been made perfect
> uniquely equipped and prepared as Savior and
> retaining His integrity amid opposition, He
> became the source of eternal salvation an eternal
> inheritance to all those who obey Him...
> (Hebrews 5:7□-□9 AMP).

My prayer is during our waiting seasons (that may feel like an eternity), that we ask for God to give us supernatural insight into those around us. When we intentionally live with God's eyes we, undoubtedly, will spend time lamenting for our family, our neighbor, our block, our community, our city, our state, our country, and for our world.

As an added bonus, I truly believe the more we become "others focused," and grieve the weight and gravity of others' sins and hardships, the shorter our waiting period will feel because our eyes will be off our circumstances.

And, remember, because our God-sized purposes are never connected to or about us, learning to lament and grieve for others connects us with those we're called to reach. During the wait, download a burden from God.

Repeat Offender

When leading it's also imperative to never count people out. I thank God He is a God of second, third, fourth and more chances. Where would I be if He had not been patient with me!

When I worked in the courts and while directing a recovery program there was a term we used: repeat offenders. Within the context of the court, this meant juveniles who recidivated or were re-arrested. In the recovery program setting, a client was called a repeat offender when she relapsed and wanted to come back into the program.

All I can say is, "Yuck!" What a terrible connotation with no compassion – labeling someone an "offender."

Yet, aren't we all offenders? And aren't we all equally masterpieces in God's eyes? What a great conundrum!

I remember one particular woman who asked to meet with me. She wanted to return to the program for the fourth time after a long battle with PCP that caused her to lose custody of her children. The latest time she left the program it was obvious she loved God and was desperate.

But she didn't want to accept the consequences of something she'd done. So she left.

It devastated me watching her walk out the door that day because I knew there was so much more inside her. Within the year, she returned to meet with me and was practically begging to come back. We were the most functional family she'd ever known.

I met with staff and, notwithstanding objections, I made an executive decision as the director to allow her back into the program. I rarely ever went against the team but there was something different this time.

In meeting with her, I discerned a difference. She had one final chance with the courts before her parental rights of her children would be terminated forever. I am so grateful I trusted the Holy Spirit's nudging to allow her to return, over the objection of many.

Fast forward to today? This woman finished the year-long program, got accepted into our subsidized housing program, regained custody of her children, and had her case closed in juvenile court for parental neglect. While life may not be perfect (it never is), she's living a life connected to God and learning how to be the best mother for her boys.

Lesson? Never count people out! Learn to mourn with people and cast out the "repeat offender" tendency to dismiss people because the power in the blood of the Lamb, Jesus Christ, can break through offenders to mold masterpieces. So proud of you M.R.! The best is yet to come, in Jesus' name!

CHAPTER TWENTY
Working through the Wait

Finding Meaning in the Mundane

I remember during the waiting period I felt so stagnant, lazy, and stuck. By nature, I'm a planner and action-oriented, so waiting runs counter-intuitive to my DNA. As a Type A personality, too, I'm very driven by outputs and outcomes.

Through the span of time, I've learned the results won't always be immediate, especially the further we are in our faith journey. We won't see the fruit of our labor expeditiously. There's a process designed to break our need to control how we arrive at the end result. God doesn't measure productivity the same way we do.

Be obedient to the minuscule tasks at hand and watch God supernaturally write the sequel. It won't happen with business as usual. The calling on our lives will entail sacrifice and will be scary. There will be temptations to control the process and be distracted by easier ways.

Speaking from experience, no matter how we try those easier ways, if it's not God's will, it won't work. Don't get distracted by assignments that weren't sent by God. And don't get distracted by the lack of money in your account.

There is a process to our God-given platforms. When we get there, people will covet the anointing – but they won't want the process. For those facing extreme challenges right now, be encouraged that your current status is the process to your platform.

Don't pray away the process. Embrace the plan. It won't unfold in a typical way. It will feel foreign and stretch every fiber of your faith.

And just because we're waiting for God's full plan to materialize, doesn't mean we have to stay still and not work during the wait.

When I moved to Memphis I was on an assignment that had nothing to do with human trafficking, which was part of my calling and destination. I knew a lot about trafficking in Chicago because I lived there many years. I had worked in law enforcement specializing in programming for girls who were exploited, conducted outreach for years, and supervised a human trafficking safe house.

When I moved to Memphis I had no connections and knew nothing about the local areas where human trafficking commonly take place. While I wasn't earning a living advocating for girls, in my free time I began educating myself about human trafficking in Memphis specifically. I created spreadsheets with all the venues and started conducting some online outreach to girls trafficked locally.

Meanwhile, I was obedient to the immediate assignment God gave me, even when it felt like I was moving backward. During this season I learned to humble myself and find meaning in the mundane as well as work toward the greater calling while I waited for it to take shape.

I didn't know why I created outreach routes and mapped every strip club, brothel, and hotel in Memphis. But I took the time to create them and prayed over every venue and person engulfed in darkness. A year later my pastor allowed me to launch a human trafficking ministry at our church. By then all the legwork had been done. I trained a team who are now meeting twice a month and the ministry is thriving because of my obedience during the wait.

The bigger picture may not make sense, but use this time to prepare for what He has revealed. It may feel insignificant and tedious. It may not produce tangible results right now. But when God asks, walk in blind obedience. There is a supernatural purpose in the mundane.

Building a Nest

One hot Tennessee summer there was a pair of small beautiful birds who constantly flew into an overhang on the back patio of our house. There was no ledge on the overhang but they were repeatedly bringing something in their beak and smearing it all over the wood post.

I watched them day after day doing this same repetitive mundane task and was so perplexed. Little by little the twigs and mud they were regurgitating started to protrude outward from that post. Eventually, their tedious project formed half a nest that stuck to the ledge wall.

It made no sense to me when they first started because normally a nest is round and built on top of something. This bird dwelling was built with no bottom support and stuck to the side of a wood post.

They were diligent at work for around a month. Then one day I open the door, see eggshells on the patio floor and hear the melodious babies chirping inside their safety nest!

These little birds worked during the waiting to prepare for the birth that God had planned for their nest. Can we say the same? Are we building a nest right now for God to birth

145

the dreams that will soar upon arrival? Start preparing.

Do you know how long an elephant is pregnant? Asian and African elephants are pregnant almost two years and their baby weighs 230 pounds at birth! An opossum on the other hand is pregnant 12 – 13 days but their average life span is only two – four years. Greatness takes time. Stop rushing.

Digging Ditches

My all-time favorite verse about preparing while we wait is found in Second Kings 3. In the story, we find three kings who join together on a journey to fight the King of Moab, who was rebelling against Israel.

In deciding which route to take, the kings settle on going through the wilderness or desert of Edom (verse 8). This desert was an especially vicious path. It was brutally hot, with very little water, and high rates of evaporation.

After seven days in these extreme conditions, the armies had no water for themselves or their animals. In their moment of desperation, the King of Israel asked to consult with a prophet.

Notice the King didn't ask God for advice prior to entering the battle. Once in a jam, only then did he seek a prophet to hear God's wisdom. Great take away: always consult with God in navigating through war to know when, where, and who to take with you.

The prophet Elisha came to the kings and asks for a harpist. "While the harpist was playing, the hand of the Lord came upon Elisha" (2 Kings 3:15 NIV).

Worship ushered the hand of the Lord in the middle of the desert valley, where the army was thirsty and tired. If you're waiting for your destiny and find yourself in a rut, be encouraged to follow the prophet Elisha's wisdom, and worship in front of the mountain.

In their worship, the word of the Lord came:

> This is what the Lord says: I will fill this valley
> with *pools of water* (2 Kings 3:16 NIV, emphasis
> added).

I especially love the King James Version:

> Thus saith the Lord, Make this valley *full* of
> *ditches* (2 Kings 3:16 KJV, emphasis added).

Great, logical, word Lord! Dig ditches in a dry and
parched land where water never comes and when it does,
evaporates instantaneously. The logic gets better:

> For this is what the Lord says: You will see
> neither wind nor rain, yet this valley will be filled
> with water, and you, your cattle and your
> animals will drink. This is an easy thing in the
> eyes of the Lord; he will also deliver Moab [their
> enemy] into your hands. You will overthrow
> every fortified city and every major town...The
> next morning, about the time for offering and
> sacrifice, there it was-water flowing from the
> direction of Edom! And the land was filled with
> water (2 Kings 3:17-18, 20 NIV).

If we continue reading, they also conquered their enemy
as prophesied.

During my most desperate times of waiting, this battle
encounter encouraged me to work through the wait. God
doesn't expect us to just sit and wait for all the lessons to be
learned and not prepare.

Seeing the supernatural requires action. God asked the
armies to take action and <u>dig ditches</u>. And not just a few

ditches. God told them to have a valley full of ditches.

God, in His infinite power, could've miraculously made ditches for the supernatural rain He was going to send in the hottest desert. But there was something about the people putting their faith into action by digging the ditches themselves. They were preparing for what God prophesied would come, meaning they trusted in His promise.

Picture them digging, maybe all through the night, sweating and parched. Imagine the conversations. I bet some were cynics and others doubters who whined and complained.

Yet, it was prophesied that the arrival of the water would defy man's reason. God said there wouldn't be any wind or rain! The water filling the valley would be supplied supernaturally by God.

If it would've rained or there was wind, the people could have explained away God's miracle for the water appearing. God wanted to make sure He got their attention through the water filling the valley without any explanation but a miracle. God received all the glory.

As we worship through the wilderness, pray to receive clarity from the Lord with specific actions He wants taken to prepare for the supernatural rain He will send.

While waiting, still prepare. Whatever assignment God gave you, become an expert. Don't wait until God calls you to move into your dreams to learn all about where you're going. God's an advance planner. Remember He's given you a womb assignment to birth new things.

When we work during the waiting season, we will already have some of the work done when He exits us out of waiting. All the work we do during the waiting will be valuable to the assignment in the dream. God wastes nothing.

CHAPTER TWENTY-ONE
Having the Right Posture to Hear from God

Discerning God's Voice

I often get asked: "How do you know it's God speaking to you and how do you know what His will is for your life?"

In my experience, in order to hear God's voice and His direction, I need to be in the right posture. I'm more adept at hearing and discerning God's voice and will, the more I'm positioning myself in His presence in complete surrender.

Some of us get frustrated, anxious, and overwhelmed because we don't know what direction to take. We expect God to speak to us but we're so busy fretting, we cannot hear His voice. Or we clearly hear but we don't like what He's saying, so we keep asking.

My children have this terrible, annoying habit of asking me something and when they don't like the answer they keep asking over and over. It plays something like this:

Child: Mom can I have a piece of candy.

Me: No. It's morning, you haven't eaten breakfast, and you're not having candy for breakfast.

Child:	(Pause. Looking with a puppy face) Mom, can I PLEEEASE have a piece of candy?
Mom:	Changing the look on your face and saying "please" doesn't change the answer. No.
Child:	(In an angry more forceful voice) Mom that's not fair!!!! X, Y, Z (plug a sibling's name in there) got one and I didn't.
Mom:	(No words necessary. Just the, "are you kidding me, the answer is still no" look.
Child:	(Softer again with puppy face resurfacing) Mom, please, please, please, please, please, can I have a piece of candy?"
Mom:	(My classic last line) The answer doesn't change, the more you ask and the more you say please. The answer is still going to be no. In fact, if you keep asking and asking and asking, you will have to wait longer for the next time you get the privilege of eating candy. You won't have candy or treats for a month!

Unfortunately, I think we have the same posture with God. We try to convince or change His mind. We sound like a broken record in prayer when He has already made His will clear.

News flash: God doesn't need our advice. He's omniscient (all-knowing), omnipresent (everywhere at all times), and omnipotent (all-powerful). In contrast: we know nothing, can barely be present in our present, and our power can't move a king size bed from one wall to another in our room without help.

The longer I've been on this journey, the more I realize I know absolutely nothing. I used to think I knew it all and acted like I could give some great counsel to God. How arrogant!

The older I get, the more I realize I'm clueless and His will is so much better than anything I could ever conjure up. So I may as well submit to the process.

I believe having the right disposition means starting from a place of total humility, surrender, and sacrifice.

I'm a practical kind of girl, so let me share some common ways in my journey that I've been able to discern God's voice. I'll elaborate on a few through the following channels:

1. The Word of God
2. Others' sharing (sermon, friend, stranger, family, book, blog, post)
3. Prayer and fasting
4. My physical senses (sight, hearing, smell, touch, taste)
5. Dreams (mine and significant others)
6. Signs and circumstances
7. The audible voice of God
8. Visions

Once they've been articulated it's easy to see how all of these require being in the right posture of being totally submitted to God? If we are so busy that we don't make time for any of these, how do we expect to clearly hear from God?

If we want to discern His voice and know His plans, we need to commit our ways (thoughts, actions, attitudes, perspectives, time) to the Lord. "Commit your works to the Lord and your plans will be established" (Proverbs 16:3 NASB).

And not just any method of being in God's presence. When was the last time sacrificial time was spent in His presence to hear and discern His voice? Are we putting the same amount of effort into this relationship with Jesus and expecting higher understanding, discernment, and wisdom? If we want a higher perspective, our sacrifice has to be higher.

As a preface to the Lord's prayer in Matthew 6, Jesus gives this instruction:

> But you, when you pray, go into your inner room, close your door and pray to your Father who is in secret, and your Father who sees what is done in secret will reward you (Matthew 6:6 NASB).

When I get in my "secret" place, where it's just me and God with no agenda and no time frame, hours can pass in prayer and reading His word. I've entered His presence possibly with one state of mind (anger, frustration, confusion) and exited His presence filled with the total opposite – love, patience, and clarity.

Only pressing into His presence sacrificially can get me to a higher place of discerning His voice. If we want more discernment, spend time with Him. As the above scripture promises, He sees what's done in secret.

Another extremely helpful practice is to have a journal when you spend time in God's presence. This way, when He speaks, you can memorialize and refer back to what you hear. Many parts of this book came from words revealed in His presence that I obediently wrote down in countless journals, not knowing it would later become a book.

When we continue to lack clarity, it's time to either be still and wait for the next word, or press in and seek higher ground. Just because we don't hear and have a lack of clarity doesn't necessarily mean we are doing something wrong and are being punished. It may just mean be still and wait.

Unless there's higher ground we can climb to hear His voice.

Higher Ground

One day I was walking into a park that has an outdoor amphitheater-style area that overlooks a large pond. My goal was to descend down the hill to sit by the water for my morning reflection. During the season of huge transitions, I was seeking God's direction. I didn't want to mess things up and make the wrong move or decision. I, therefore, spent more time in His presence so I could hear from the Lord.

Standing on the top level of that amphitheater, I realized a higher vantage point existed from where I was standing looking down at the water. As I walked down the sloped area closer to the water, I pray aloud: "As I go and spend time with you, GOD, give me a higher perspective. Give me a new word. Not a word that you spoke to me yesterday. But a word specifically for today from a higher perspective."

Let's pause and ask God to take us to a higher level of discernment. Increase the ordinary measures we've been taking to hear His voice. Double whatever level we were engaging in among the eight common ways listed to hear His voice. For example, if our routine is to pray for twenty minutes at night before we go to bed, add twenty minutes at the beginning of our day.

We'll need to remain intentional because the enemy exploits whatever he can to stop us from increasing our discernment. He wants us to remain confused and overwhelmed.

Fight back and carve out time. I know we're busy. Trust me I'm a working professional with three small children, a husband, a home, lead a ministry, and write.

It can be done.

We may have to cut some things that are dear to us, but it

will be time well spent. For those with the DNA of go, go, go, go, go please make sure to read on until "The Art of Rest."

Some of us know God is trying to say something, and we blatantly ignore His prodding. It's like getting a notification for a new voicemail, knowing it's there and who it's from, but ignoring it and never listening. If you're like me and terrible at playing voicemails, with time they come up for automatic deletion, with me never even hearing them.

I wonder how many notifications God has sent to me but I wasn't listening to His "voicemail" and I missed the message. God pursues us but He is also a gentleman. He will not force His will on our lives. We have free will to respond.

CHAPTER TWENTY-TWO
Discerning God's Voice

Patterns and Obedient Peace

Ponder this simple but revolutionary truth. We get to a point in our journey with God where He develops a pattern in the way He speaks to us. The way God speaks and reveals things to me may not make sense to any other person and most of the time it is way beyond the reasoning of this lawyerly brain.

There were many times where I fought, questioned, or reasoned with His "patterns." Yet, God has such an amazing track record. Even when I habitually fail to pursue His disciplines, He continues to yield discernment. I'm so grateful for His unending grace and consistent way of speaking so specifically to a wretch like me.

We are empowered to build healthy development in our walk with God.

What does it mean to hear God speaking through consistent patterns? A pattern is a recurring sequence of responses. For example, this may sound odd but God speaks to me a lot through signs: street signs, signs in windows, etc.

When I left my comfort zone in juvenile court, there were times where I questioned whether I had made the right decision. I learned Egypt will always be calling me back.

Shortly after leaving the secular workforce for full-time ministry, I saw a huge orange construction sign with the words: "Fresh Oil." The road had just been paved and the wording on this sign was how they were alerting the public.

Well, God spoke to me through that rare sign, telling me He had fresh anointing oil He was going to pour on me because of my obedience and faithfulness.

God is a God of peace and clarity. When we don't have peace about something, be still. When revealing His will, there's almost always a confirmation. He is a confirming God.

We will see the same message confirming how God feels about a situation. Especially if you're stubborn – like this Dutch girl. He has to hit me over the head and tell me the same things, sometimes over and over, for me to listen.

However, the more seasoned I've gotten, the less often this takes place because I have become familiar with His patterns. And God has the best track record. I trust He only wants the best for me.

When you start discerning the patterns in the way God speaks to you write them down. In fact feel free to write some in the margin. Then you should analyze what patterns you are reinforcing with your responses.

The level of peace we'll experience is commonly connected and directly correlated to our level of obedience. If we're in a place of obedience, even when all hell breaks out around us, it won't matter. We will still have peace because we're being obedient and in God's perfect will. It's when we're disobedient to God that we have no peace and experience turmoil.

When we have a decision to make and we have no peace, err on the side of caution and don't make any decision. God doesn't speak in confusion, turmoil, restlessness, or anxiety. If that's where you find yourself and the decision can wait, let it wait.

He will meet us in the higher ground we create for Him and speak to us recognizably.

Holy Spirit Within and Multitude of Counselors Outside

> As for you, the anointing which you received from Him abides in you, and you have no need for anyone to teach you; but as His anointing teaches you about all things, and is true and is not a lie, and just as it has taught you, you abide in Him (1 John 2:27 NASB).

I will share this next piece of wisdom with some caution. Sometimes we become so busy asking our friends, family, pastors, and spouses what they think God is trying to say and we fail to tap into the Holy Spirit that's within each of us as believers.

This scripture reminds us the anointing of God abides in us and will teach us about all things. When we devote time to be in God's presence He teaches us. We need to seek God and allow Him to speak to us through His Holy Spirit and anointing within us. We don't need to shop around and talk to everyone until we get the answer we want to hear.

I share this with caution because this truth doesn't mean we don't need each other. We were created for relationship. God made woman because it wasn't good for man to be alone (see Genesis 2:8).

First John 2:27 isn't a license to isolate ourselves and only rely on the Holy Spirit and anointing within to teach us. Yes, we need to discern God's voice through the Holy Spirit within us, but we also need to discern when to seek wise counsel. And the counsel we seek should then be filtered through the Holy Spirit to ascertain whether it's wise.

There needs to be a balance. There is a danger when relying exclusively or too heavily on what everyone else is saying, and failing to consult with the Holy Spirit within ourselves. At the same time, we cannot shut out wise counsel from others and isolate ourselves. Proverbs (the book of wisdom) instructs this:

> Where no counsel is, the people fall: but in the multitude of counselors there is safety (Proverbs 11:14 KJV).

So when we seek counsel from others, how do we know and discern what they are telling us is God's will? The key is to have what I call a "word filter."

Word Filter

Once we allow others access to speak things into us, I believe a "word filter" is imperative. Some things spoken to us aren't from God and can be highly deceptive. Remember sheep-wolves?

We need to be careful and have discernment.

Having a "word filter" allows things to either clash with our spirit (in which case, let them bounce right off us) or confirm what the Holy Spirit within us has taught or is in the process of teaching us. One question to ask: does the counsel confirm or conflict with what God's Holy Spirit anointing has taught us?

Remember how we spoke about being selective about whom we share our God-sized dreams with because not everyone can handle them? In the same way, we need to be discerning about whom we let speak into our lives. We have to discern His voice among those whom God is sending to us – beware of those sheep-wolves!

My circle tends to get smaller and smaller the older I get. When I was younger I had scores of friends. Now I have my spouse and a few confidants who I let see my complete vulnerability. I have my husband and a friend, Stephanie, who are my armor bearers. They know me intimately. I can share things with them knowing they're going to speak over the other voices that are lying or trying to deceive me. They're my biggest cheerleaders, and I give them access and permission to say the difficult things.

This access and intimacy have only developed over time.

CHAPTER TWENTY-THREE
Silent Years

Silence

No matter where you are in your journey with Christ, we will all experience periods where God is silent. It's in His nature.

When Jesus was on the cross, He was separated from His Father when He got the keys to hell and paid the price for our sins. We hear Jesus' agony during this separation that equated to utter silence: "About three in the afternoon Jesus cried out with a loud voice… "My God, My God, why have you forsaken me?" (Matthew 27:46 NIV).

After His death there were three days where His loved ones did not hear from Him. There was silence. His physical body had no life, no breathe, or blood pumping through His body. The only thing left in the tomb was His lifeless body.

I can only imagine how confused and disappointed His inner circle felt. What about all the promises? What about everything they encountered and witnessed walking alongside Him? None of it made logical sense. It wasn't the way they thought it would end. After all the miracles, silence. Stillness. In the silence, their Messiah lay mocked and dead.

Jesus was silent when He was falsely accused. Jesus was silent when they flogged, whipped, and beat Him beyond recognition. At the sound of His voice He could've called legions of angels to fight His accusers and sidestep the cross. But He choose to remain silent for the of salvation man.

He walked down the Via Dolorosa, bloody and in pain. Out of love for me and you, He remained silent to become the sacrificial lamb for our sins.

While the tomb was silent for three days, death could not hold Him (see Acts 2:24). After His silence and the stillness in the tomb, He had the final word. In three days His silence became our weapon that the gates of hell cannot prevail against. Jesus' accusers did not take Jesus' life. He gave it, humbly…silently.

So maybe God is silent right now and you don't sense His presence. Jesus died a brutal death in silence. During the waiting years of silence, I was challenged to ask myself what needed to die. What was a stench to God?

There were seasons of silence where I believe God had nothing left to say to me until I killed the things that He wanted to purge out of me, so I could move forward. My waiting was self-inflicted. I caused the delay with my lack of obedience.

Popped Eardrums

Remember that encounter with Bell's palsy described earlier caused by shingles in my ear? The pain was so incredible and during the process, I lost hearing in that ear. One night after intense time in His word, I got up and started warring in prayer. All of a sudden, BAM, my eardrum popped. A huge gush of sound resounded in my ear.

The pop was accompanied by an incredible amount of pain, but at the same time brought much-needed relief – relief of pressure that had built up and also a relief to hear more distinctively. I was able to hear things from that ear that before were completely clogged and blocked. Equate the sensation to when you're done flying somewhere and our ears pop back to normal. Now multiply that intensity times 1,000.

This experience reminded me of how we can become so clogged and blocked off from hearing even a whisper from God in our ear. We've all held our nose and blown out to try and pop our eardrums. Imagine if we were to ask God to "blow" all the things that are clogging us from hearing what He was trying to whisper in our ear.

Many things can cloud our hearing: sin, busyness, negativity, selfishness, pride, unforgiveness, bitterness or another barrier that's prohibiting us from truly hearing or discerning God's voice. Don't over-complicate it. We will hear Him if we remove the barriers. It takes intentionality.

> Your ears will hear a word behind you, 'This is the way, walk in it,' whenever you turn to the right or to the left (Isaiah 30:21 NASB).
>
> My sheep hear my voice, and I know them, and they follow me (John 10:27 ESV).

Falling Asleep in Mediocrity

Silence has the capability of pushing us towards or further away from God. One day I was sitting in church and saw one of the worship leaders sleeping during service. It got me thinking. How many believers are in church sleeping spiritually?

We go, serve in ministry, but because of long periods of

waiting on God we've settled for mediocre Christianity. What happens to our fervor during seasons of stagnancy? Good intentions won't carry us through those seasons of waiting. There's an old nature that must die in the silent years. Can we believe when in the battle and there's no orders? When God is silent? Do we remain on fire for God or do we grow cold? Worse still, lukewarm?

Some aren't hearing from God because you fell asleep and aren't in His presence regularly enough now to hear His voice. Wake up and get back in the race. Some things are not manifesting because we haven't activated our warfare and faith. We haven't drawn on all the weapons of mass destruction we discussed earlier. We've in effect prolonged the waiting like the Israelites in the dessert for forty years who never saw the promised land.

Birthing in the Silence

While you may not be able to hear or see God, He is birthing something in the silence. When a mother is pregnant with a baby, she doesn't see or hear her baby. Yet, the baby is growing in her womb. The baby is silent.

Now yes, we've created all these new gadgets with technology to hear the baby growing (heartbeats, ultrasounds). But normal everyday experience does not entail physically hearing a baby crying while in the womb. A woman can sit in a meeting with a top executive while pregnant, because the baby's screams cannot be heard. But we know they are developing and being nurtured.

Oh, but when the baby is born, what is the first sign that doctors look for to make sure the baby is alive and well? A scream, as if to say: "HERE I AM WORLD!"

In the same way, just because God is silent does not mean He is not birthing something extraordinary in you and me.

God knows the future. Trust silently in His eternal perspective. Don't stop in the wilderness. Keep walking towards all God has for you. Keep the future in your focus (see Jeremiah 29:11).

Ponder this: Noah only got the assignment to build the ark once. He didn't need constant reminders and pep talks. People were probably ridiculing him while he built it because there weren't any signs of rain. He didn't need to be reminded by God of his assignment. He held on to what God told him once, and he was obedient. Through his obedience God re-birthed and re-populated the earth and made an everlasting covenant.

Some of us hear a word from God and we are inspired and confident. Then a week passes by and we begin doubting and are discouraged. Learn to trust God even in the silence. There were periods where God spoke so profoundly to me through His silence. Those silent seasons built even more faith for me to trust in what I heard and knew and to push through in worship, adoration, expectancy, and anticipation.

Enduring Faithfulness

I recognize there are many today feeling discouraged because you've had the right posture but you still aren't hearing from God. The devil may be deceiving you to think you're doing something wrong.

If you have the right posture and are seeking God's face and going to war during the waiting, rest assured, God is not punishing you.

During those seasons of giving everything we have while holding on by a thread in silence, clutch to the last thing you heard from God. Grip it for dear life. Trust and believe in the last thing God did tell you. Write it down and put it everywhere as a visual reminder to drown out the other voices trying to deceive you that you're forgotten. Whatever voice is louder will take root. God is working behind the scenes while you wait.

You may be praying for a wayward or child. An addiction may be gripping a loved one. Keep praying! Regardless of the length of the wait, hold on to the last thing God said.

God is a professional Finisher so rest in "being confident of this, that he who began a good work in you will carry it on to completion until the day of Christ Jesus" (Philippians 1:6 NIV). God always finishes what He started. He doesn't leave things half done. Waiting becomes bearable when we activate our trust and faith in a sovereign, all-powerful God.

What He has for those who wait is beyond what any of us deserve or can even visualize in our feeble minds. "No eye has seen, no ear has heard, no heart has imagined, what God has prepared for those who love Him" (1 Corinthians 2:9 BSB). So wait expectantly and hold on when He begins answering your deepest longings.

As you lean in, He hears your cry. Rest on this promise:

But as for me, I will look to the Lord; I wait for the God of my salvation; my God will hear me (Micah 7:7 ESV).

Lastly, if you've been obedient, are waiting for a miracle, but haven't yet fasted, I encourage you to tap into this most neglected weapon of mass destruction. The miracle you are asking for may be tied to the supernatural and not the natural and requires prayer and fasting (see Matthew 17:21 NASB). In a fast we intentionally deprive our flesh to gain a spiritual objective. There is a war between the flesh and spirit. In a fast we eliminate our flesh which allows us to clearly commune with God and hear His will and His voice in an undivided way. Read Isaiah 58:6 for the powerful results we reap when fasting with the right posture.

CHAPTER TWENTY-FOUR
Dreams, Visions, and Audible Voice

Discerning God's Voice through Dreams, Visions, and Audible Voice

God speaks to His children through dreams, visions and audibly at times. We find all these modes of communication in the bible and God still uses them today. In fact, we should experience them to a higher degree today if we believe we're in the last days:

> In the last days, God says, I will *pour out* my Spirit on all people. Your sons and daughters will prophesy, your young men will see visions, your old men will dream dreams (Acts 2:17 NIV, emphasis added).

I believe we're living in the days of a fresh outpouring of God's Spirit on the young and old, manifested through prophecy, visions, and dreams.

Dreams

There are so many biblical examples of God speaking in these ways. My favorite is Jesus being revealed to His earthly father, Joseph, through an angel of God speaking to him in a dream.

> ...an angel of the Lord appeared to him in a *dream* and said, 'Joseph son of David, do not be afraid to take Mary home as your wife, because what is conceived in her is from the Holy Spirit. She will give birth to a Son, and you are to give him the name Jesus, because He will save His people from their sins (Matthew 1:20-21 NIV, emphasis added).

Prior to this dream, Joseph was going to leave Mary when he found out she was pregnant before marriage.

For those with the gift of prophetic dreams, have a paper and pen by the bed and have a dream journal to document the date and details of dreams. Fight the urge to fall back asleep and take the time to quickly preserve your dreams in writing.

The interpretation may not make sense when we first receive a dream. It may, in fact, feel random at first. That's why it's so important to preserve all our dreams because we may not receive the interpretation until a different time and season.

In addition, God may give us a dream that has nothing to do with us, and when we share it with the one for whom it was intended, they will know exactly what it means.

I don't dream much but I know a woman who has prophetic dreams all the time. One night I was asking God for clarity on something I was feeling in my spirit and I asked God to give this woman a dream that night that only I would understand. The next morning I called her and asked her what her dream was about the night before. When she told me her dream I knew precisely what it meant.

She was shocked. She felt like the dream was random because it meant nothing to her. I explained how I had asked God to speak to her in a dream. Again, this is all something that a logical lawyer would not believe is true. However, through the patterns in my life, I know without a shadow of a doubt God speaks through dreams.

This is just one example.

My husband saw me and my father in several dreams years before we met and were married. When he saw me years later, he knew I was going to be his wife because of the dreams. You'll have to read the book he will publish someday to hear that amazing testimony of his dream girl come true!

Visions

I have also had visions while awake. Now before I'm labeled crazy and people think I have problems with hallucinations, go back to Acts 2:17 about God giving people visions and dreams in the last days.

I was doing laundry one day and folding clothes. I asked God for wisdom about who our keynote speaker should be for the nonprofit I was directing at the time. I looked up and I saw a woman with a masquerade ball mask on.

She was one of the women who graduated from the program we facilitated but I couldn't tell which one. I just knew that God's keynote for that gala was the women we served. They needed to be front and center and they were going to wear a mask and unveil the truth on the atrocities that were plaguing our girls, women, men, and families.

I presented the idea to the staff and one of the former

graduates on staff agreed to be the keynote speaker. When she came to the podium that night she was wearing a beautiful mask exactly like the one I saw in the vision. She eloquently shared all the masks she had worn throughout her life.

When she unveiled the mask and took it off, she spoke of the freedom she had received in Christ through the program they were supporting that night. There were tears throughout the room and a standing ovation. God showed me this keynote speaker in a vision.

God spoke to many people in the bible through visions. Here are just a few examples:

> ...the word of the Lord came to Abram in a vision: 'Do not be afraid, Abram. I am your shield, your very reward' (Genesis 15:1 NIV).

Tell me, who is the "word of the Lord"? It was Jesus Himself who appeared to Abram!

> And the Spirit lifted me up and brought me in a vision by the Spirit of God to the exiles in Chaldea (Ezekiel 11:24 NASB).

> As they [Peter, James, and John] were coming down from the mountain [after the transfiguration], Jesus commanded them, saying, 'Tell the vision to no one until the Son of Man has risen from the dead' (Matthew 17:9 NASB, parentheses added).

> And the Lord said to Paul in the night by a vision, 'Do not be afraid any longer, but go on speaking and do not be silent; for I am with you, and no

man will attack you in order to harm you, for I have many people in this city' (Acts 18:9-10 NASB).

Audible Voice

God can speak to His children in an audible voice.

> As soon as Jesus was baptized, he went up out of the water. At that moment heaven was opened, and he saw the Spirit of God descending like a dove and alighting on him. And a voice from heaven said, 'This is my Son, whom I love; with him I am well pleased' (Matthew 3:16-17 NIV).

There are many other examples in the New and Old Testament, where God spoke audibly to His children. Here are just a few additional well-known examples:

- God called and spoke to Moses from within the burning bush (see Exodus 3:1-4).
- God gave Moses the tablets and told Moses he must not see His face, only His back (see Exodus 33:23).
- God called Samuel's name while he was laying down and Samuel thought it was the prophet Eli (see 1 Samuel 3).
- Jesus knocked Saul off his horse on the road to Damascus and asked why he was persecuting Him (see Acts 9:4-6; Acts 22:7).
- Adam was given instructions in the garden concerning what they could eat and God asked both Adam and Even who had told them they were naked (see Genesis 2:15-17; 3:10).
- Jesus brought Peter, James, and John up the mountain and, during the transfiguration, God spoke and confirmed Jesus was His beloved Son (see Matthew

17:5).

For we did not follow cleverly devised tales when we made known to you the power and coming of our Lord Jesus Christ, but we were eyewitnesses of His majesty. For when He received honor and glory from God the Father, such an utterance as this was made to Him by the Majestic Glory, "This is My beloved Son with whom I am well-pleased" – and we ourselves *heard this utterance* made from heaven when we were with Him on the holy mountain (2 Peter 1:16-18 NASB, emphasis added).

Stewardship of Revelation

When God reveals things through a dream, vision or prophecy it's our responsibility to steward them according to God's will. In my experience, God wants us to respond in one of three ways when He reveals something to us:

1. Prayer and intercession,
2. Sounding the trumpet or alarm, or
3. Preparation so we are ready.

After I get a revelation, I always ask God, "You just revealed this to me; now what do you want me to do with it? Pray, sound the trumpet, or prepare and brace myself?"

Let me explain. I believe sometimes God reveals some things so we can pray and intercede for whatever or whomever the revelation is about. For example, maybe God revealed that someone is going to get fired from their job. After we seek God, He may ask us to pray for the aftermath and provision for the person.

In other situations, God reveals things to us so we will sound the trumpet and share the dream with the appropriate person. Take some time to read Ezekiel 33 about our calling to be watchmen and the consequences if something is revealed and we don't warn that particular person.

Maybe God revealed that someone is living in sin and He wants to send us as a prophet so they can be set free and come out of the darkness, in the name of Jesus. These are called words of knowledge that only the Holy Spirit can reveal to us and speak through us.

Assignments to sound the trumpet can be extremely difficult. And the more we're obedient when asked to sound the trumpet, the harder the assignments will become because God knows He can trust us with deeper revelations.

I believe God reveals things to many, but not all are obedient to deliver the message for various reasons. They may be fearful of the consequences, fearful of the person, concerned or doubt whether they are hearing correctly, among other things.

Lastly, sometimes God reveals something to us so, when it happens, we will not be caught off guard and we'll be ready. One example of this relates to a residential program that was very near and dear to my heart for years.

God showed me through a dream that it was going to shut down for various reasons. My first reaction was I wanted to go sound the trumpet and tell my leader so we could fix things and not have it close down.

My husband gently said to me, "Kaitrin, if it's God's will for this program to close, it will happen no matter what you do and no matter what you say. Maybe He's revealing it to you so you can mourn now so that when it happens you're strong for the staff you're managing."

That's exactly what happened. I mourned and wept. It closed within weeks and I was able to provide the necessary counsel to the staff who ultimately had to be laid off.

Because I had advance warning, I had recovered from the initial shock and was in a stronger place to minister.

So the next time you're shown something, take the time to hear from God about what He wants your responses to be.

PART THREE: THE ART OF REST

CHAPTER TWENTY-FIVE
The Art of Rest

Before we enter into the last phase of knowing when to exit the waiting and preparation phase, let's discuss the importance of what I call "the art of rest." Knowing how to rest is central to serving effectively in ministry and helps us avoid the trap of over busyness.

Diligent Rest

I've seen and been trapped myself by a scheme of the enemy which I believe is rampant in the church today, busyness. This observation comes from two decades of being a volunteer in ministry, serving full-time in various ministries, and working and consulting with churches around the nation on events and outreaches.

This is not meant to be a personal attack on any specific church, but instead a general observation for our current day and age.

While trapped in busyness I was ensnared in such a deceptive plot. I justified it by telling myself, "We're busy doing the things of the Lord, so it's okay." I moved from one event on the calendar right into the next, with no rest in between.

For those with workaholic and results driven temperaments like me, the danger of waking up trapped in busyness is even greater. We tend to find our identity in what we're busy doing. It's becomes less about who we are working for (Jesus) or why we are working. While subtle, it can reflect idolatry when our identity is tied to the work and not the Master.

> Therefore let us be *diligent* to enter that rest, so that no one will *fall*, through following the same example of *disobedience* (Hebrews 4:11 NASB, emphasis added).

Hebrews challenges us to "be diligent" to enter into rest. Other versions describe the action to enter into rest as: "make every effort" (NIV), "do our best" (NLT). But my favorite is the King James Version that instructs us to "labour" to enter into rest.

In other words, it will take work to enter into His rest. It's not an oxymoron that we have to "work to rest." It's the truth.

We must act with intentionality and effort to not become so busy that we forget to enter His rest. Otherwise, we lack the energy and desire to come into His presence and we forfeit that rest.

How often are we too tired to spend time in prayer because we're giving God the sloppy leftovers at the end of the day when we barely have anything left to give? According to this scripture, we have to "make every effort," "do our best," "be diligent," and yes, "labour" to enter into the rest that God has for us.

Rest is not the absence of work pressing to get done. Rest assured (no pun intended), there will always be work needing to get done. The bible promises we will always have the poor (see Matthew 26:11). There will always be people who need that Holy Spirit conference you're busy planning, that life-changing outreach ministry that you're working to expand, or whatever "God project" or secular project that's keeping you from entering His rest.

Hebrews 4:11 (as well as Hebrews 3:18, 4:6) even explains why we need to enter into rest. If we fail to rest, we are being disobedient and will fall.

Go back and re-read the scripture. I like to think of it this way: resting is the conscious decision to temporarily press pause so, when it's time to hit play, we're dancing to the right beat and not out of step.

God doesn't need the rest. The rest is for us – so we won't fall. I don't believe God rested on the seventh day of Creation (see Genesis 2:2-3) because He was tired. He is omniscient and omnipresent. He doesn't get tired. While we sleep, He's awake. I believe He rested to be an example for us and maybe to pause and admire His beautiful creation.

So today go spend some extended time in His rest, and I promise all that needs to get done will be there in the morning. And maybe, just maybe, we'll be more effective because we've rested in the Almighty's presence.

Rest doesn't just mean getting sleep – although that's part of it. Rest has the deeper meaning of making time to be in God's presence, being still and getting filled with His strength – strength that'll be needed when it's time to work again.

When we fail to rest in His presence, essentially we're working in our own strength. I've learned a valuable lesson in the most taxing seasons. I get more done in one hour resting in God's presence than I can when I work eight hours in front of a computer planning something for the Kingdom.

In no way does rest mean being lazy. That's a different root altogether. If you find it difficult to rest, rebuke the lie that you're being lazy when you are honoring the Sabbath.

Getting to the Root of Busyness

Why do we struggle to rest? What is the root cause? That's what God is after, the root. Maybe some of us don't like rest because it creates a quiet space that really forces us to deal with difficult things, while busyness allows us to escape having to face those hard realities. We choose to avoid it.

Others struggle because they see themselves as a commodity and have the notion they have to do things for God in order for Him to love and be proud of them.

Or still, maybe we find ourselves so driven by success and achievement that busyness is our way of accomplishing great things in order to be recognized or valued by others?

Lastly, some are busy carrying loads they have no business carrying. I was driving in Chicago one day on a busy street and there was a local moving truck that said, "Objects being lifted are heavier than they appear."

It made me think, with all my busyness, what heavy objects am I lifting that aren't mine to carry? The bible tells us that His burden is easy and His yoke is light. Let God lift the load. It's not our burden to carry.

These are just a few of the roots I've observed in others and battled to overcome myself.

Whatever the reasons for our busyness – God seeks the core of why we struggle with entering into His rest. Not resting and failing to honor the Sabbath is a sin. And I have news for us – if we don't rest – my experience is God will force the rest He commanded upon us.

Either we'll get sick or injured, and physically will be forced to rest. Or God will strip us of all idols and take our ministry away. Ouch! Yes, ministry can become an idol.

Labor, be diligent and make every effort today to rest in His arms today. Not just in our "normal" ways. Press in harder and deeper than we ever have. When we enter this type of radical rest, we will come out ready to work with the power and authority that we could never have achieved in our own strength.

In our present age, we also need resting places to recharge our batteries so we operate in a position of power, filled with the Holy Spirit. So, frequently visit the places where you can feel at home with the Lord, not just your prayer room but also quiet open places where you can worship in the midst of nature.

V-Pattern

As winter approaches, have you sometimes looked in the sky and seen migrating birds? You would have noticed that these birds always fly in a V-pattern formation. One bird flies at the tip of the V and the rest span outwardly: this helps spread the resistance of the wind.

They even take turns being at the point of the V, the place of most resistance, and work together as a team so the journey is less taxing. In this way they are able to travel further working as a team.

I will get to the application of the V-pattern in a moment. But here was my problem.

I'll be honest because it's a root I had to break at one time. Some people don't know how to rest because they're control freaks and don't know how to delegate. As a recovering control freak myself, I understand this phenomenon. I wanted things done a specific way, and when I delegated things, I ended up having to do them again myself because it wasn't done exactly the way I wanted.

As our enterprise expanded , I kept up with this domineering mentality which meant longer hours and less time with my family. Eventually, my controlling spirit took a toll on my family and my health. And, honestly, it all stemmed from an arrogant and prideful root. I was basically saying, "I know best and no one can do things as well as me."

I learned how to relax, let go, and build up and be part of a team. I invested time in people, teaching them how I needed specific things done and why. Letting go was often painful and meant letting people use different wording or complete the assignment differently. But more than that, it meant shedding my ego.

The shedding paid off – in essence, I learned the art of empowering people and letting them grow from their mistakes. I, too, had to learn to depend on people. And, in the process, I was taught new and often better ways of accomplish things than if I'd controlled everything. I'm still learning in this area and am grateful for all the lessons gleaned in the waiting of letting go.

If you don't learn this skill, at times when you face resistance and obstacles, you won't have a solid team to help push you through the resistance and get to your destination.

What does all this have to do with knowing how to rest? When we learn to delegate, build a team, and empower other people, we will mentally and emotionally find rest and be more at ease because we know there's a team behind us.

The greatest leaders surround themselves with others smarter than themselves and do not feel threatened or jealous. I've seen and experienced a controlling spirit rooted in a fear that others would "outshine" them. Their need to be seen in everything oppressed and limited others because they feared being bypassed in some way.

Rest assured, what God has for us no one can take away. As empowering leaders, we need to be secure in who we are in Christ and release others into their different callings.

Let's learn to adopt a V-pattern leadership style and utilize our combined resistance to the wind.

Distracted Rest

> I say this for your own benefit, not to lay any restraint upon you, but to promote good *order* and to secure your *undivided devotion* to the Lord (1 Corinthians 7:35 ESV, emphasis added).

It was 11:30 at night and I felt my 9-year-old daughter gently tapping me awake and whispering she couldn't sleep. I rub my eyes and ask her what's wrong, expecting to hear she had a nightmare or was thinking about something that troubled her mind.

No. She tells me there was a fly in her room that was buzzing around her and keeping her awake. Really?

I had sent her to bed at 8:30 p.m. and her rest was distracted for three hours by some pesky fly buzzing every time she tried to fall asleep? So I had to march right up there with a fly swatter and smash the distraction so she could get some peaceful rest. True story.

Many of us suffer from not being able to rest. Just like this annoying fly, whenever they get ready to rest, they lie awake distracted by something that is troubling their mind. Maybe the distractions are due to being a workaholic, or maybe because of an excessive worry with a mind that finds it hard to settle down, or maybe it's just a tendency to be easily distracted…or other reasons.

Well, whatever the reason, rest is a biblical mandate and, not honoring the Lord's Sabbath day of rest, is a sin. So we shouldn't be surprised that one of the enemy's tricks is to keep us busy, distracted, and without rest. That's why one of the worst and most deceiving traps I fell into was not resting because I was so busy in ministry.

Working "for the Kingdom" doesn't always mean God told us to do it, especially if the work takes us away from our intimacy with Him.

It wasn't until I became unemployed for an extended period of time and wrote this book that I truly learned the power of rest. Never in my adult life had I been off work for so long! I didn't know what to do with myself.

In retrospect, for the first two months I was in such shock that all I could do was go every day to a nearby park. There I would journal and meditate on God's promises literally from 9:30 a.m. until 2:30 p.m.

Sitting watching ripples form in the water from fish life beneath became my full-time occupation. It was a great time of resting in God's presence and even when there was so much falling apart around me, I was coming to a place of supernatural peace resting in God's promises.

There was no Wi-Fi at the park. So the first couple of days it was somewhat annoying because I couldn't stream worship music, look up a scripture when I was reading the word or, to be honest, quickly check my texts or emails in the five hours I was there.

To be frank, by the third day, I really started to appreciate the uninterrupted time I had with God with no phone, no computer, no emails, no texts – no distractions. It was just me and God. The wonderful thing was that during this unobstructed rest this book was birthed and the national nonprofit I was destined to lead was formed.

These two months of my life entailed unprecedented time with my Savior. While you may not have the luxury of taking months off work to be in His presence, we can all build a space in our every day busy routine where we power off our phones and rest in God's presence with no distractions.

After returning to the regular busyness of life I look back at that sabbatical as a defining moment and can't wait to be back there. In the meantime, I have a full-time job, three small children, a husband, a business, and a ministry. Finding rest is possible, necessary and required if we are going to accomplish God-sized dreams.

We have to be intentional and make our rest a priority, which does not mean trying to balance all the things in our lives. Prioritizing doesn't mean balancing. We aren't called to be a juggler and move things around to make sure they're all balanced. If we find balance, we'd look like we're in the circus.

The difference with prioritizing means we have to cut something so we have time for something else, in other words, specifically resting in God's presence.

Some of us need to go get our fly swatters out and kill the fly in our room that's trying to distract us from the rest we need. With it, we'll be much more effective and beneficial to those in our spheres of influence.

PART FOUR: KNOWING YOUR EXIT

CHAPTER TWENTY-SIX
Knowing your Exit: Uncomfortable Nest

So how do you know when the waiting and preparation season is over and it's time to transition into the destiny God has for you? The worst thing we can do is wait for all God's promises and, when it's time to enter, stay stuck beyond the period God intended. We need to know our exit.

Stirring the Nest
God will begin stirring the nest when He is calling us to step out of the waiting and preparation mode and into our divine destiny. In my experience, it wasn't an instantaneous experience: poof – waiting over, and poof – living in my dream.

There was a transition period. There was a space where I was out of the waiting and preparation period and I was moving into the fullness of my purpose.

I believe the beginning of my waiting ended when I left the juvenile court in 2013 and went into full-time ministry. A year later, God began speaking to my husband that our time to move again was near. I'd just stepped down from my position at juvenile court and began directing the nonprofit of my dreams. I didn't understand how my husband could be hearing it was time to leave when I had waited ten years to be in my then current reality.

I had sacrificed everything, stayed obedient, and now my husband was telling me it was time to leave?

Add to this scenario this little complication: my husband didn't know where we would be going. He only knew God was calling us outside the nest.

Great!

No clarity and no plan. Again, for this logical lawyer, not a good recipe for major life changes. Then things started getting uncomfortable in ministry.

When an eaglet is born they don't know how to fly. They are dependent on their parent for everything. Their parents make their nest extremely comfortable and safe for the egg and then for the newborn eaglet. As the baby gets older and more independent, the parent eagles begin taking some of the padding and cushioning from the bottom of the nest to make it poky and uncomfortable.

So then the eaglet waddles around in the nest, poked by twigs and feeling the pain. This pain motivates them to come out of the nest and practice flying with their parents. In a short time, they are soaring in the manner in which they were destined.

Do you find yourself getting frustrated and uncomfortable in your current setting? Pray and ask God if He is stirring the nest and wanting you to "mount up" (see Isaiah 40:31).

If we're experiencing frustration and hurt, don't be so quick to rebuke the devil. It could be God assigned that very person for the specific purpose of causing frustration in our lives.

What?

God put them there to hurt and attack me?

Yes.

God knew the only way we will leave the nest and soar is if we're so offended and so hurt that we have no other choice but to leave. So that very person who we feel assassinated our dreams, in actuality is handing us an opportunity. In economics it's called "opportunity cost." Handed to you is an opportunity to leave the nest and soar into undiscovered airspace. Don't be bitter at them. Shift your sights and thank them.

Round Peg in a Square Hole

I have witnessed many people staying in the waiting and preparation season longer than what God intended. This stalling happens for many reasons, some of which are:

1. Fear of the unknown, failure, and/or rejection,
2. Doubt as to whether we heard correctly or whether God is able,
3. Flat out disobedience and rebellion – we want to do what we want to do,
4. So comfortable and safe – we don't want to take a risk,
5. So blinded or distracted that we miss God's signals that it's time to transition into His destiny.

Working in a government position I saw so many people get comfortable. I often wondered if God had more for some who just went through the motions. Had they got stuck in the waiting period that maybe was only meant to be training ground? Throughout my career I've heard many people say: "I will do what God really called me to do when I retire."

It's not that some aren't called to the positions they're in. They absolutely are. However, some unfortunately get comfortable and miss the growth opportunity. They remain in a place instead of launching out. To everything there is a season.

When I gave two weeks' notice so unexpectedly, I remember countless people telling me they were inspired and wished they had the fortitude to follow suit. When I reflect on all God has accomplished since I resigned from my comfort zone, I often wonder what my life would be like right now had I not stepped out in radical faith.

When we find ourselves not fitting into the culture or place where we're currently planted, don't make the mistake of trying to force a round peg into a square hole.

Celebrate that you are a peg and they are square, and ask God if He wants you to be a peg there or move on. He is a confirming God. If He calls you to move on, it has nothing to do with them necessarily. Your destiny might just not be tied to them.

We aren't called to fit in. We're called to stand out. If we're to be imitators of Jesus, recognize that He didn't fit into the culture of His day, so bound by tradition. He broke through the culture. Let the organization or business we don't fit in be full of squares and let us be the peg God called us to be.

If being the one peg in an all square setting is not best for all parties, then know your exit. Don't change into someone you aren't. Again, it's not about being right or wrong; it's about being in God's perfect will and knowing your exit.

Eagle in a Parakeet's Cage

If we keep ourselves in a place where we aren't called, we'll begin to feel trapped. I'm sure all of us have been in a situation where someone was jealous of us or threatened by us. Perhaps that's where you find yourself today.

When the jealous people are our peers/equals it's difficult and usually accompanied by a lot of backstabbing and deceitful slandering. Even more difficult is when the jealous person is our supervisor or, God forbid, our ministry leader.

In an earlier chapter I mentioned how I spent a season battling this dynamic with a supervisor who even told me he was jealous of me. I didn't even have to discern the jealousy. He flat out told me.

The season under this supervision consisted of anything I touched being critiqued, misunderstood, or oppressed. I was outside my comfort zone and in an environment that was anything but empowering.

As time passed, I experienced more and more criticism, isolation and oppression. I began sinking into a rut. Deep down I knew there was so much more in me and I began going stir crazy sitting in a cubical day after day.

During this season, I humbled myself and daily (sometimes hour by hour) had to purify my heart and choose not to grumble or complain. I wasn't going to let myself spend the next forty years in the wilderness because of the wrong posture.

I was in this position after sacrificing God's call He revealed years previously at that leader's conference. My obedience required great sacrifice, trust, and leaving everything I knew and cherished. And despite my sacrificial obedience, I found myself in an oppressive environment.

I have news. Just because we're obedient to what God is telling us to do, doesn't necessarily mean life will get easier. In fact, in my experience and, biblically speaking, things will usually get harder once we're obedient. We'll need thicker calf muscles for where God is taking us to sustain the weight of the calling on our lives.

Just look at what happened to Moses when God told him

to go to Pharaoh. Moses was reluctant, but eventually he obeyed. And every time Moses went to Pharaoh as God instructed to plead for his people, God hardened Pharaoh's heart, causing judgment and suffering through the plagues. Obedience was followed by rejection and oppression.

When I was finally released from the jealous grip of oppression, I was wounded, hurt, and insecure. Do you find yourself there? Good. That's right where God wants you so He can put you back together. Now that your heart has been tested and bruised, you are ready to soar.

Months after the release from oppression, I found myself in a meeting with a pastor and, without disclosing any details to him, explained I was coming to his ministry scarred and wounded.

I will forever carry this seasoned pastor's wise response in my heart and pray it blesses anyone who is in a similar situation who feels oppressed and discouraged. He described my extended time in a cubicle in this way: "You were an eagle in a parakeet's cage."

After meeting me for the first time, this pastor immediately released me from that restrictive parakeet cage. He commissioned and empowered me with immediate assignments and handed back one of the gifts God had gifted to me.

He asked me to teach a three-part series in a bible study. With that assignment he challenged me this way: "I don't want you to teach Kaitrin. I want you to minister to the women and start a revival." I literally felt a flicker being re-ignited deep within my spirit, broken and wounded as I was.

My sister, my brother, you may feel trapped in a parakeet's cage right now where you're being oppressed. But at heart you know you're a mighty eagle who was meant to soar. You didn't ask for the anointing, but for some reason He has entrusted a high calling to you.

Ask God for the lessons He has while you're confined to a parakeet cage. Above all else, remain humble to oppressors and, when God opens the door for release from the cage – know how to exit and take off.

Soar and let go of the hurt the jealous oppressor inflicted while in the cage and vow to say those two words we learned earlier: never again!

In retrospect, the parakeet cage was how God transported me for a brief moment out of my comfort zone and into the new promised land where I had no idea I was going. Sound like Abraham?

He transported me in the parakeet's cage to my new Promised Land, and on arrival, He released me. When I walked out of the cage, God allowed a short restoration period to strengthen my wings that had been cramped during transport. Now firm-footed and ready, I was positioned to soar, all for His glory.

> But they who *wait* for the Lord shall renew their strength; they shall mount up with wings like *eagles*; they shall run and not be weary; they shall walk and not faint (Isaiah 40:31 NASB, emphasis added).

One thing's for sure. Don't let the dreams, promises, and call die while you're waiting and being transported in the parakeet's cage. Yes, there are even lessons in oppression! Don't miss them and don't get comfortable and spend years in the parakeet cage. It wasn't built with us in mind as a permanent home, but was meant for a small transporting season to get us to the place where we were poised to soar.

CHAPTER TWENTY-SEVEN
Knowing Your Exit: God's Perfect Timing

Anticipated Seasons

So how will we know when it's time?

We all know that the leaves on trees begin to change beautiful colors in the fall. I used to ascribe these changing colors of fall to the weather. However, moving to a southern state in the U.S., I noticed the trees in October were beginning to change colors even when the weather wasn't cold.

I didn't understand how they knew without a visible change in the weather that fall was coming. It was as if they anticipated the seasons.

In fact, leaves don't begin changing colors because of colder weather. They change colors because the days start getting shorter. With less sunlight photosynthesis shuts down and chlorophyll dwindles. Chlorophyll reflects the green in leaves, and when it subsides, the color of the leaves change and they eventually die. Good science lesson?

This got me thinking. I wonder if we can anticipate an end to a season when our days are getting shorter in whatever assignment we're in? And then I remembered my husband anticipated the change coming when he told me, right after I arrived at what I thought was my destiny, that God was calling us out of the nest. He was tuned in and God began preparing him for the change.

We have to be alert to all that God wants to share with us in one season that will transition us to the next. Just like the trees, we can anticipate the death of one season that will bring life to the next. Our anticipating, like the trees, also requires exposure to the s-o-n – Jesus.

Distracted Assignment

One trick of the enemy is to try and distract or side-track us when our transition into all God has for us is near. The distraction may come in nice packaging, but it may not be God's perfect will for us. It is meant to draw us away from His real assignment. "Let your eyes look directly forward, and your gaze be straight before you" (Proverbs 4:25 ESV).

One day I was leaving to run an errand and left my 11-year-old son with an assignment to sort and put clean laundry away. Knowing my son, I left him specific step-by-step instructions that sounded something like this:.

Step One – Bring all the clothes into the living room (so he had a larger space).
Step Two – Sort the clothes by person they belong to (necessary with a family of five).
Step Three – Sort the clothes by type (those that need to be hung, those that go in drawers).
Step Four – Hang those that need hanging and fold those that go in drawers.
Step Five – Put them away in the right person's room.

Even with this level of detail, my analytical son still had questions. Two hours later when I returned from my errand, my son was laying on the living room floor, on step two throwing clothes into different piles, having made this task into an elaborate basketball game. Did I mention he had two hours to finish the assignment?

You see, he got distracted. He probably spent 30 - 45 minutes collecting hangers in people's rooms by "inventing" a hanger holder with a lacrosse stick. He then probably spent 40 minutes finding supplies and making signs for each person's "basketball station" where he could throw – I mean sort – the clean clothes.

Now don't get me wrong. These qualities are some of the things I absolutely adore about my son and I chuckle as I write. He is creative, an inventor, extremely analytical, and like most 11-year-old boys, hates chores and likes playing sports and having fun.

Yet, every gift has an Achilles heel. These great qualities of my son also come with his tendency to make a huge project out of everything and also to be easily distracted and sidetracked.

God is a God of order and He has assignments for each of us to steward. Are you someone who is dependable, consistent and gets your assignments done diligently without distractions? Or are you someone whose gaze looks all over the place and loses focus, making it difficult to complete assignments? If you're the latter let's talk practically.

First, acknowledge that you struggle in this area and resolve that you want to get better. Second, you may think it was a little demeaning or over the top that I gave my son five steps for the simple task of putting the clean laundry away. However, I am trying to teach him to break a task into manageable steps and to stick to these steps as his guide to stay focused.

My suggestion is become a list person. Have paper and pen (or, if younger, your phone) with you wherever you go in case you get an assignment and need to take notes. Keep them in one central place and not all over the place. Refer back to this list and prioritize the items there.

Some things are more time-sensitive; some may take longer and may have sub-parts of things that need to take place to get that one thing done. Once you complete tasks, cross them off. Be careful not to get sidetracked with your time and steward it well.

And, yes, like my son – create small ways to have fun within the tasks but don't let things overtake you to the point where you lose sight of your goal and become ineffective.

We also need to be alert because some assignments will probably be presented during our waiting seasons that may be a distraction from the enemy. Remember, not all assignments, even when they're to serve in the Kingdom, are God's perfect will for moving us into our destinies.

Learn to discern (using the tips from the earlier chapter) which assignments are from the Lord and which are distractions.

The assignments that are called to distract us will usually come looking for us, packaged in irresistible boxes.

Exit Timing
God's timing is perfect. We don't want to exit the waiting and preparation period too early and not receive all that God has for us to learn. Remember God doesn't waste anything and things we're learning in the waiting seasons are needed where He's taking us.

In addition, we don't want to stay stuck in the waiting and preparation period beyond what God intended. Don't stay in the parakeet cage longer than God assigned.

In summary, don't exit too late or too early. And don't assume it's time to exit just because you're frustrated where you are, knowing there's more inside of you. God could be teaching you how to humble yourself and stay committed even when you don't like the assignment or the people. If I had left juvenile court prematurely when I got the assignment over fiscal responsibilities I would've missed all those lessons and skills. I had to push through the mundane and frustration to learn.

Leaving the waiting and preparation season into the fullness of our destinies will require radical faith. We will not have all the answers. We will be terrified, yet have peace – if that even makes sense. It will probably go against everything we learned growing up. It will not be logical. And it will, most likely, require money and resources that we don't have.

While we may have complete clarity on the final destination of God's call on our lives, we probably will not have much direction on how to get there. We may have to let go of financial security in the way man provides. I went from depending on man for my six-figure paycheck (that as I got closer to the dream started to shrink) to depending on God to deliver my salary.

Extremely scary! But if faith was easy, you wouldn't need faith.

Again, while in the place of exit I only had a small understanding of what God wanted as my next step. Earlier in my walk, I found God gave me more information because my faith muscles were not built up. He guided me in a clear, concise way. The longer I served the Lord and trusted in His patterns, the higher my sense of discernment and trust in the Lord became. Simultaneously, the less God revealed to me, the more He was showing me how to trust and believe in Him at higher and deeper levels. I was eating solid food.

> But blessed are your eyes, because they see; and your ears, because they hear. For truly I say to you that many prophets and righteous men desired to see what you see, and did not see it, and to hear what you hear, and did not hear it (Matthew 13:16-17 NASB).

The closer we are to the exit, the lonelier it may get with those around us, who won't understand. But, the more intimate we will become with our heavenly Father. During this season of only having a small amount of direction, I intentionally focused on what I did know, even if that was minute. I didn't focus on all the things I didn't know, which would've caused unnecessary worry and conjecture.

Today, focus on that next step He is leading you to take. Don't even think of two to three steps from now because when you step into your destiny you probably won't know those steps. It's the deepest level of faith you've ever experienced. But no worries. All the lessons in the waiting and preparation which built those faith muscles, will be carried into your next season.

Remember, when I wrote this part of the book, I had been off work for months and the only clarity I had was to write. I didn't know why or what I was supposed to write or the purpose. I just knew I needed to write, so I started journaling. The next thing I knew, 45 days later, the writing supernaturally led to this book.

We were living on a small cushion and the longer I wrote,

the more our finances were dwindling. By the time I was at the end of the book writing this chapter, our regular bank account was almost depleted.

So logic told me to go get a job, but God was telling me to continue radically trusting in Him. With each day of utter dependence on the Lord, I was walking into uncharted waters. Only in these uncharted waters would I experience uncharted miracles.

The unseen, unknown, and miraculous will only be reached by radical faith, obedience, putting our hands to the plow, and putting in the work. Today, I choose to move beyond my regular patterns into the supernatural and I ask God boldly for His promises to be established:

> And now, Lord, let the promise you have made concerning your servant and his house be established forever. Do as you promised, so that it will be established and that your name will be great forever. Then people will say, 'The Lord Almighty, the God over Israel is Israel's God! And the house of your servant David will be established before you' (1 Chronicles 17:23-24 NIV).

Don't stay stuck and crippled by fear, doubt and whatever else is causing you to not exit.

> So Joshua said to the sons of Israel 'How long will you put off entering to take possession of the land which the Lord, the God of your fathers has given you?' (Joshua 18:3 NASB).

When it's your time to exit, go in and seize the land He has given you!

Let's Do This!

The manifestation of your God-given dreams is on the other side of radical faith in action. Don't just say He is a God of the impossible. Act out this belief by the way you live your life. Radical faith will not make sense or be logical, nor is it based on the way you feel. Action faith will produce your miracle and fulfilled dreams.

After years of waiting, now I don't hate it. I now know I need it, I actually embrace it, and I want to live a life full of waiting in expectation for what God has for me next.

Appendix

Character Goals to Carry into our Destiny:

Sincere and genuine

Thoughtful

Consistent

Reliable/Dependable

Joyful

Hard Working

Generous

Loving

Compassionate

Flexible

Faithful

Creative

Trustworthy

Honoring

Respectful

Even-tempered

Independent

Self-initiated

Efficient and organized

Responsive

Humble

Teachable

Character Flaws to Purge or Temper while Waiting

Bossy and overbearing

Argumentative

Grouchy

Sneaky

Restless

Greedy

Selfish

Complaining

Competitive

Oppressive

Jealous

Gossiping

Dishonest

Disrespectful/rude

Impatient

Fearful/afraid

Prone to panic/anxiety

Doubter

Sarcastic

Unresponsive

Unhealthy

Poor with finances

Unorganized

Procrastinating

Sexually immoral

Proud

Picky

ABOUT THE AUTHOR

Kaitrin E. Valencia earned her BA in Criminal Justice and Sociology from Ohio Northern University and her JD from the Chicago-Kent College of Law, Illinois Institute of Technology. She was admitted to the Illinois State Bar in 2003 and Tennessee Bar in 2018.

Kaitrin worked in Chicago's Juvenile Court from 1999 – 2013 where she was a Deputy Chief and Legal Advocate in the Juvenile Probation and Court Services Department.

From June, 2013 – 2016 Kaitrin was Executive Director of the Chicago Dream Center, a Christian non-profit with 14 different ministries focusing on outreach, human trafficking and housing that included 94 beds for society's most marginalized individuals.

Upon moving to Memphis, Tennessee, Kaitrin launched a non-profit, Skyway Railroad, in 2018 with national reach to reach those bound in modern day slaveries.

Kaitrin has a passion for writing and teaching. She was an adjunct professor at City Colleges of Chicago where she taught and mentored students entering the criminal and juvenile justice fields. She regularly speaks at church retreats and conferences and taught a weekly class to women in the human trafficking and recovery program she led.

Kaitrin has published articles, has a Christian blog, and published a riveting book, *Voices Outside the Stadium* documenting her encounters with human trafficking during the week of the National Football championship game.

When not consulting, writing, or advocating for under-resourced families, Kaitrin loves road trips and spending time with her husband, Emilio Valencia, Jr., and three children. Visit her at kaitrinvalencia.com and skywayrailroad.org.

54809921R00129

Made in the USA
Columbia, SC
07 April 2019